GHOST STORIES

VOL I & II THE HAUNTED LOCATIONS AND PARANORMAL ENCOUNTERS COLLECTION

H.J. TIDY

External Content:

H.J. Tidy assumes no responsibility for the persistence or accuracy of URLs for external or third-party internet websites referred to in this publication and does not guarantee that any content on such websites is, or will remain, accurate or appropriate.

Designations:

All brand names and product names mentioned in this book and on its cover are trade names, service marks, trademarks, and registered trademarks of their respective owners. The use of these designations is for identification purposes only and does not imply any endorsement or association with the book or its publisher. By reading this book, the reader agrees to abide by the copyright laws and the terms and conditions stated in this notice. Any violation of the copyright terms may result in legal action.

TABLE OF CONTENTS

ENTER THE REALM OF THE UNKNOWN

WELCOME TO THE CAPTIVATING WORLD OF "GHOST STORIES: The Haunted Locations and Paranormal Encounters Bundle," where reality entwines with the supernatural, drawing readers into a realm of spine-chilling tales. I am H.J. Tidy, your guide on this thrilling journey through haunted locations, ghostly encounters, and unexplained mysteries.

In 2016, my fascination with the paranormal ignited an irresistible urge to share strange and lesser-known tales that had captured my imagination. Thus, "Ghost Stories Vol I" was born, presenting a compilation of haunting accounts and paranormal events that intrigued me endlessly. These stories evolved beyond mere narratives, offering captivating insights into the haunted locations and the eerie ghost tales associated with them.

Each visit to a haunted location further beckoned me into the alluring world of the supernatural, fueling my insatiable curiosity for the mysteries lurking within these eerie places. These haunting encounters inspired my choice in "Ghost Stories Vol II," where I now center exclusively on the haunting legends shrouding these places. This second volume boasts an even more diverse array of haunted tales, brimming with accounts of encounters that challenge conventional explanations.

Now, I invite you to join me on this enthralling journey of genuine encounters with the paranormal. Together, we will traverse haunting locations worldwide, delving into eerie manifestations that challenge our understanding of the unknown. Brace yourself for spine-tingling mysteries that transcend the boundaries between the living and the dead, leaving us questioning the limits of human comprehension.

Let's enter the extraordinary world of "Ghost Stories," where the ordinary transcends into the supernatural realm, and reality intermingles with the unknown. As we uncover the enigmatic secrets within these haunting tales, prepare to be both thrilled and unnerved, for this captivating collection promises an unforgettable exploration of the supernatural and the inexplicable.

GHOST
STORIES

A COLLECTION OF THE WORLDS SCARIEST HAUNTED LOCATIONS, PARANORMAL ENCOUNTERS, AND DEMONIC POSSESSIONS

VOL 1

H.J. TIDY

INTRODUCTION

GHOST STORIES HAVE ALWAYS BEEN A PART OF HUMAN CULTURE. They appear in different forms throughout the world, even playing critical roles in many ancient legends. They have long been the subject of famous pieces of literature and appear in great works such as Emily Brontë's *Wuthering Heights*, Bram Stoker's *Dracula*, and William Shakespeare's *Hamlet*. But are these stories merely fiction? As with most myths, there is generally a seed of truth to be found. Take the legend of Dracula as an example. This is based on an actual person named Vlad III, who was a Wallachian ruler in the 15th century. He was infamously known for impaling his enemies and prisoners of war on giant stakes, and some legends say he dipped bread in their blood and ate it.

For many centuries, people believed in ghosts and the paranormal without question. But what exactly is a ghost? The answer to that question is not simple, as different worldviews influence our belief in the spiritual world. Nowadays, many people do not believe a spiritual world even exists. However, those who believe in ghosts classify them as spirits or apparitions of a person or animal that died and still inhabits the world. They appear in many forms, from translucent beings that appear as shadows floating in the air to more solid but still shadowy phantoms with discernable features.

In this book, we will look at some spooky stories recorded from around the world and supported by compelling evidence. We will examine a few examples of supernatural events in each of the following types of stories in this book: ghosts, haunted locations and objects, and poltergeist activity.

So sit back, get comfortable, and get ready to enter the world of Ghost Stories.

CHAPTER 1:
JUSTICE FROM BEYOND

T
HE TRUTH WILL COME OUT ONE WAY OR ANOTHER. NO MATTER HOW HARD WE TRY, it will always reveal itself. It may take time— sometimes centuries. But in the long run, one can never hide from the truth. In the case of the Greenbrier Ghost, the world saw evidence of this. The paranormal facilitated this coming out of the fact, and it was the ghost herself who convicted her murderer.

In 1873, Elva Zona Heaster was born in Greenbrier County, West Virginia. Her early life and childhood years remain a mystery with little documented information. But we know she was pregnant in her teens and was a mother out of wedlock at age twenty-two. The fate of the child remains unknown. In 1895, Elva and her family met with the man who would eventually become her husband, Edward Stribbling Trout Shue.

Edward was a blacksmith who recently moved to Greenbrier County in search of a better life. Elva, also known as 'Zona', was raised in Richlands, a town in Tazewell County, Virginia. Edward was a breath of fresh air she never encountered before. He attracted her attention almost immediately. After their initial meeting, Zona frequently returned to the blacksmith shop to see him, and eventually confessed her feelings for him. Their romance was like a Harlequin whirlwind affair.

Their union, however, did not please Zona's family. Her mother, Mary Jane Heaster, was against it. She instantly disliked Edward and said there was something strange about him. But there was little she could do, and eventually, the couple married, becoming Elva Zona Easter Shue. They began their life together in their log house. After that, things quickly fell apart.

Three months later, on January 23 1897, Edward went to the market. He sent his neighbor's young boy, Andy Jones, to check in on his wife and see if she needed anything. Andy did as he was told and entered the Shue household. However, as Andy walked through the front door, he faced a scene that no little boy should have to.

As Andy passed through the front door, he stumbled upon the dead body of Mrs. Heaster. She was lying at the foot of the stairs, lifeless. Her body was positioned unnaturally, lying with straight legs pushed together, one arm resting across her chest, and the other positioned to her side. Her head was tilted to the side. Her eyes were open, staring up at Andy. The boy crept towards her lifeless body and whispered her name. When his quiet "Mrs. Shue?" received no response, he realized something was seriously wrong. He panicked and ran home to tell his mother. Fearing the worst, the woman called for the local doctor and coroner, Dr. George W. Knapp. It took Knapp almost an hour to get to the Shue house after receiving the call. Strangely, by the time he arrived at the house, Zona's body was missing.

Minutes before Dr. Knapp arrived, Edward had returned home. He carried his wife's body up the staircase to their bedroom, dressed her, and laid her body out. This was odd because, in those days, it was the lady's job to wash and prepare a body for internment. However, Edward demanded he wanted to prepare his wife for her burial. So he dressed her in a high-necked dress with a stiff collar, placing a veil over her face.

Dr. Knapp then examined Zona's body. He noticed slight bruising around her neck. As he went in for a closer look, Edward burst into a fit of tears, reacting almost violently, crying as he held Zona close to him, making it difficult for Dr. Knapp to perform a thorough examination. Edward then yelled at the doctor, becoming extremely agitated.

Dr. Knapp did not want to aggravate him any further. Based on Edward's visible grief and lacking signs of foul play, Knapp concluded the cause of death to be an 'everlasting faint'. Later, he changed the official determination to 'childbirth'. Before her death, Zona was under treatment for 'female trouble', which was strange because no one knew whether she was pregnant. For whatever reason, Dr. Knapp went with childbirth, closing the case. It is possible she was trying to get pregnant and consulted with him for advice.

Dr. Knapp needed to inform Zona's parents of her passing and arrange for her burial. Two men who were friends of Zona volunteered to go out to Meadow Fluff and inform the family. It took a while, since they lived about fifteen miles away. When they finally got to Mrs. Heaster, she seemed more angry than sad, almost expecting this news. Finally, she spoke out, saying, "The devil has killed her."

The funeral was set the next day, on January 24 1897. Hanley Undertaking placed Elva Zona Shue in an unfinished coffin and drove her by carriage to her home. There, she laid in wake through Sunday and into the next morning as friends and family showed their respects.

""Interestingly, Zona's husband acted oddly during the wake. He showed utter devotion to his wife and was extremely protective of her body, in a manner that came across as almost psychotic. He kept close watch over her, always hovering by the open casket, not allowing anyone else to come close, not even her parents. He would let no one touch her, especially when he put a pillow on the side of her head. His behavior was notably erratic. His demeanor alternated between grieving loudly and painfully for his wife and suddenly becoming extremely energetic and delighted.

Apart from the pillow, he placed a rolled-up sheet on the other side of her head and tied a long scarf around her neck. The pillow and the sheet, he claimed tearfully, would aid his wife in her final rest and make her more comfortable. The scarf was her favorite item of clothing, and it was his farewell to her, even if it did not match the burial dress she was wearing.

That Monday, Zona's body was taken to the local cemetery, the Soule Chapel Methodist Cemetery. As she was moved, people noticed a strange looseness of her neck. People gossiped about theories, but there was nothing they could do because Knapp had ruled her death to be natural.

Additionally, Edward was generally well-liked and respected by the community. No one openly questioned his strange behavior. Most saw little beyond a grieving husband.

But from Zona's mother, Mary Jane Heaster, refused to believe he wasn't to blame. She was convinced he had something to do with her daughters' death, though she had no proof. Before the burial, she took the sheet from her daughter's body and handed it to her son-in-law, who refused to take it back. Confused, she took it home with her, where she noticed a strange smell on it.

Assuming that it was merely dirty or unclean, Mrs. Heaster washed it. When she dropped the sheet into the basin, the water turned red. She noticed the sheet soaked up the color like a sponge. Thus, the sheet turned red while the water became clear. No matter how hard Mrs. Heaster tried, she could not wash the red stain off the sheet. She was sure this was a clear indication that something was wrong, and that Zona's spirit was communicating with her in a plea for help.

Mrs. Heaster began praying every night in hopes her daughter would come to her and give her a clue to prove her death was a murder. She prayed every night, and finally after four weeks, her wish was granted. It started as a bright light at first, then turned into an apparition. The room chilled and right in front of Mrs. Heaster, Zona's ghost appeared. Finally, Zona revealed the truth.

Edward was a man possessed of a cruel nature. He was prone to abusing the people closest to him and regularly beat Zona. He often had violent fits, and on the day of her death, he flew into a rage when he thought she didn't make any meat for dinner. In his anger, he snapped her neck. Then Zona's ghost spun her head all the way around to demonstrate. Mrs. Heaster was frightened beyond her wits and sat on her bed screaming. She was ready to dismiss what she saw as a figment of the post-traumatic stress she'd experienced. However, for the next four days, Zona's ghost would come back.

The subsequent visits would be different. There would be a bright light that would shine behind her eyelids, and then slowly, a mist would solidify into her dead daughter's sunken corpse while the room became utterly cold. These appearances continued until Mrs. Heaster finally realized this was the proof she was waiting for. Now the challenge was finding someone who would believe her.

Mrs. Heaster went to the local prosecutor, John Alfred Preston, and asked him to reopen the case. Reportedly, she spent several hours with him in his study, arguing to convince him. Preston sat politely, listening to her story. Understandably, with a ghost story as her only proof, he was hesitant to reopen the case. He was sympathetic to her plight, though it seemed he might send her away. However, after contemplating the case and Mrs. Heaster's ghost story, Preston knew there was something suspicious about Zona's death.

He sent deputies to Dr. Knapp's house to question him more about what he found when he examined Zona's body. Dr. Knapp told the deputies that the examination was never complete. Edward's "grief" interfered with the examination. Preston and the Doctor both decided a new autopsy needed to be done right away. The local newspapers picked up on the story and reported that Mary Jane Heaster wasn't the only one that suspected murder. A few of the other locals stated that Edward was acting strange.

On February 22 1897, in Nicholas schoolhouse, the autopsy proceeded next to Zona's cemetery. School was called off for the children that day, and Zona's body was exhumed. Finally, everyone would discover what exactly happened her. Edward complained about attending the exhumation, but deputies demanded he be present. After telling him that, Edward arbitrarily said, "I know I'll be arrested, but they won't be able to prove anything."

The whole autopsy took three hours by the light of kerosene lamps. The cold weather had perfectly preserved the body, which made the examination easier for Dr. Knapp. He removed the vital organs first, then made an incision in the back of her neck to remove her brain. Upon going to the neck, they did not need to go any further.

Dr. Knapp turned to Edward and said, "We have found your wife's neck to be broken."

Edward dropped his head and said, "They cannot prove I did it."

The autopsy also revealed Zona's windpipe was smashed and her spine dislocated between the first two vertebrae. Finger marks around her neck indicated she was choked to death. This evidence confirmed what Mrs. Heaster already knew: Zona was murdered.

Until then, her encounter with Zona's ghost was easily dismissible as something triggered by loss. However, medical evidence proved her suspicions to be correct. Mrs. Heaster could have dreamed it all up, but dreaming the details of how her daughter died was highly unlikely. In a way, Zona called to her mother to receive the justice she deserved and her mother delivered. Police arrested Edward once the autopsy was complete and sent him to the jail in Lewisburg to await trial.

Because the evidence against Edward was not even circumstantial because it was from a ghost, he pleaded not guilty. However, more details about Edward revealed interesting details from his past. His name was not Edward, but Erasmus. He was from Augusta County and married two times before Zona. The first time to Allie Estaline Cutlip, with whom he had a daughter named Gerda. She left him with their daughter after he went to jail for stealing horses. Four years later, they divorced. In their divorce papers, Allie stated that Edward beat her multiple times. Allie's parents took in their daughter for unknown reasons.

Five years later, Edward married a woman named Lucy Tritt. After less than a year, Lucy was dead. Strangely enough, there's no record of how she died. According to Edward, she fell and hit her head on a rock. After that, he fled town. Two years later, he met Zona.

The trial began on June 22 1897. Many people came forward to testify. Mrs. Heaster was Preston's star witness. As an experienced attorney, Preston knew the idea of her daughter's ghost would not give her credibility. Therefore, he limited his questions to the known facts, expertly avoiding the ghost sightings and focusing on the truth.

But Zona's appearance to her mother instigated the entire trial. So, Shue's lawyer attempted to discredit her during his cross-examination. He tried to prove she was a liar and a cheat. Mrs. Heaster, however, knew what she saw. She staunchly defended her belief, and despite clear badgering, she would not retract what she said. It was the defense that took up the issue of the ghost, meaning the judge could not instruct the jury to disregard the testimony. The jury had to either believe or disbelieve what was said based on their impressions.

Based on all the evidence and story of Zona's spirit, the jury of twelve found Edward Stribbling Trout Shue guilty of Elva Zona Heaster's murder and sentenced him to life in prison.

On July 11, a mob of fifteen to thirty men got weapons and rope and headed toward the jail to hang Edward for his crime. Sheriffs were notified about the lynch mob and took Edward to a location about a mile outside of town. The organizers of the mob were eventually charged.

Edward had to be moved to the West Virginia State Penitentiary. He stayed there for three years until an epidemic of measles, mumps, and pneumonia went through the prison. Edward got sick and died on March 13 of 1900. There is no record of where he was buried.

For the rest of her life, Mrs. Heaster never recanted the story of her daughter's ghost. She received her justice. Mrs. Heaster never claimed to see Zona's ghost again. Whether or not the ghost appeared to her, it seems something extraordinary happened.

The State could not dismiss this. So a historical marker made of stone was erected near the cemetery where Zona is buried.

It reads:

Interred in the nearby cemetery is Zona Heaster Shue. Her death in 1897 was presumed natural until her spirit appeared to her mother to describe how her husband Edward killed her. An autopsy on the exhumed body verified the apparition's account. Edward, found guilty of murder, was sentenced to state prison. Only known case in which testimony from a ghost helped convict a murderer.

CHAPTER 2:
THE BROWN LADY OF RAYNHAM HALL

WHEN YOU RETREAT TO A PEACEFUL AND SERENE COUNTRY HOUSE IN ENGLAND, you would expect the experience to be calm and relaxing. The last thing you would expect is to come face to face with a ghost. And yet, this is what visitors to Raynham Hall encounter when they visit. The Brown Lady of Raynham Hall is quite the infamous ghost, having been sighted several times over the years, even having been photographed and published in a magazine!

Raynham Hall is a country house in Norfolk, England. It has been with the Townshend family for close to four centuries. The Hall lent its name to the five nearby estate villages, collectively known as The Raynhams, and was the backdrop for the infamous photo of the Brown Lady of Raynham Hall published in the *Country Life* magazine in 1936.

The manor is one of the most beautiful and splendid buildings in the Norfolk area. Its construction began in 1619, but it ended up being a false start, resulting in nothing but collecting a significant amount of Ketton stone in the area until 1621. It wasn't until 1622 that the actual construction began. By the time the owner, Sir Roger Townshend, passed away in 1637, it was almost finished. However, the manor remained unfurnished, some rooms not fitted out and incomplete until much later.

It was not until the second Viscount, Charles Townshend, that the manor would vault into infamy. William Kent, one of Britain's most lauded and sought-after architects and designers of that era, worked for Charles Townshend to construct additions and extensions to the manor's interior. His style is most notable in the north front of the mansion, which he aligned closely with the work of the famous architect Inigo Jones. Between 1725 and 1732, Kent built the entire northern wing of the manor. He also decorated the interiors, bringing elements of his style, evident in the aesthetically and architecturally pleasing carvings of the chimneypieces in the doorways. Even the staircase was painted to imitate niches.

To this day, if you walk into Raynham Hall, you can see the architect's style and his genius in designing the entire mansion. Not only did he create a structurally sound building, but he also gave the interiors a majestic touch. The family reinforced this by putting up paintings and portraits that would, in today's market, go for hundreds of thousands of dollars. Some of these paintings are still in the mansion today, even after the auctions in the mid-1900s. For instance, in the Princess's room, there is said to be a painting that was the preliminary sketch for Van Dyck's famous *Children of Charles I*. These paintings also include works by other celebrated painters such as Godfrey Kneller and Sir Joshua Reynolds.

For all its splendor and wonder, the true majesty of Raynham Hall lies in its history and the legend that surrounds it: The story of the Brown Lady who haunts the hallowed halls. She is called the 'Brown Lady' regarding the brown brocade dress she is seen wearing.

Charles Townshend, born in 1674, served as a leader in the House of the Lords in England. The Brown Lady of Raynham Hall is none other than his wife, Lady Dorothy Walpole, who was the sister of Robert Walpole. Robert Walpole was a statesman who is generally accepted as being the first Prime Minister of Great Britain. While people debate about the exact dates of his term, many recognize the years between 1721 and 1742 as being under his control. He holds the record for being the longest-serving Prime Minister in Britain's history. In addition, Robert Walpole was regarded as one of the first people to have integrated the rising power of the House of Commons and the diminishing strength of the House of Lords, thus attempting to establish more equality.

Robert Walpole may have been quite the gentleman, but his brother-in-law, Viscount Charles Townshend, was not. Charles was notorious for his short temper. But, despite Charles' temper, he seemed to have some luck with the ladies.

Lady Dorothy, rumored to be the prettiest of the Walpole sisters, caught the wandering eye of Charles Townshend, who was then already married to Lady Elizabeth Pelham. Charles asked for her hand in marriage, and it was not long before Lady Dorothy moved to Raynham Hall, which she would continue to haunt after her life on Earth ended.

Accounts tell us that there was a political rivalry between Walpole and Townshend, even though they were neighbors in Norfolk. Their dissension hit terminal velocity when Walpole built Houghton Hall in Norfolk as well. Townshend believed Raynham was the crowning glory of Norfolk, and any other mansion would only diminish and degrade its grandeur. He was not ready to admit the loss of power and control that came with another politician, one as strong as Walpole, establishing a base near his own.

So, was Lady Dorothy a peace offering from Walpole's side? Was she a gift to please Townshend into accepting reality and burying the hatchet? We will never know if Walpole knew he caused his sister to be collateral damage in his fight with Townshend. Neither will we know if Lady Dorothy herself was interested in or even accepted this marriage. Her motivations and aspirations were lost to the pages of history.

What's speculated, however, is that she was having an affair with Lord Wharton at the time of her wedding, perhaps even before her marriage. Lord Thomas Wharton, the first Marquess of Wharton, was notorious for his debauched and hedonistic lifestyle. Born in the year 1648, he was a nobleman who also served as a politician. But his interests lay more in drinking, partying, and leading a life of pleasure and self-indulgence. He had multiple lovers and was quite the hedonist.

Some records indicate he may have once broken into a church while drunk. Then, he sacrilegiously relieved himself against the communion table, as well as in the ''''church's pulpit. Whether or not this is true, we do not know, as there is little hard evidence that proves it. However, when accused of it in the House of the Lords, Wharton was speechless and could not offer a proper response, indicating that he was guilty of the crime in question.

What is sad is that, despite all his debauchery, he was a man of great wit, charm, and intelligence. He was one of the most influential politicians in Aylesbury, and his voice was instrumental in the *Ashby vs. White* case, which is famous in the UK for having established the right to vote and equality for all.

It is little wonder that Lady Dorothy—attracted to his wit, charm, and power—allegedly consented to be his lover before her marriage mended to Charles Townshend, and this carried on even after the wedding. However, it was Townshend's discovery of her illicit affair that led to her death.

It was not a crime of the mad, murderous rage of a jealous husband who grabs the nearest weapon he could find. It was instead a much crueler, more painful death that Lady Dorothy endured. Charles Townshend abandoned her and locked her up in the family home, left to die alone and discarded within the walls of Raynham Hall. Her husband did not even allow her to visit her children. Can you imagine being trapped in a mansion that serves as your prison with no one to interact with, thrown there by your husband, and abandoned by your lover? Lord

Wharton certainly did not try to free her or help her in any way. Slowly, Lady Dorothy probably went mad.

At that time, there was an outbreak of smallpox. When poor Lady Dorothy caught the disease, no one was there to nurse her back to health. Alone, lonely, and sick, Lady Dorothy may have gotten so weak in body and spirit she lost the will to live. You could say Dorothy was already haunting Raynham Hall even before she died. Finally, in 1726, her sickness and her soul made her so weak, she passed away and was buried on the grounds.

Another theory proposed is that Lord Wharton's wife—the famous writer, poet, and aristocrat, Lady Mary Wortley Montagu—may have caused Lady Dorothy's grief. The Countess of Wharton was allegedly in a rage over her husband's affair with Dorothy. Mary deceived Dorothy with an invitation to the Wharton estate. She conspired with Charles Townshend, and it was at her cunning direction Lady Dorothy become fatally trapped inside Raynham Hall.

Whatever the actual reasons that led Lady Dorothy to this fatal end, what is sure is that it was a slow and cruel demise. No wonder the anger within her soul ensured that she would not rest. Her spirit, still looking for vengeance or even justice, still wanders the grounds, waiting for release.

Charles Townshend himself died in 1738. He spent his last years at Raynham, possibly being haunted by the appearance of his wife's ghost. However, that was not enough for her restless spirit to move on. She was still angry, sad, and filled with pain.

The first recorded sighting of the Brown Lady happened in 1835. Colonel Loftus went to Raynham Hall to spend Christmas there. He was walking to his room late at night when suddenly he caught sight of a figure in front of his bedroom.

It was a woman dressed in a brown brocade gown. When he tried to get a better look at her face, she vanished. The next evening, she appeared to him again. This time, Loftus made a note of her empty eye sockets and her glowing countenance. When news of this haunting came out, it was no surprise members of the house staff resigned from their jobs and permanently left the cold manor.

More people told stories of their encounters with the ghost. Whether this Brown Lady was Lady Dorothy was something people did not think about. They called her the Brown Lady, who appeared and terrorized unsuspecting victims. The second reported sighting is a second-hand account. Captain Frederick Marryat, a writer, sailor, and friend of author Charles Dickens, was the next person to have seen her. While he did not comment on his experience, his son, Florence Marryat, recounted his father's brush with the paranormal.

By this time, the locals had seen the Brown Lady often enough that Raynham Hall was getting a reputation as a haunted mansion. Marryat wanted to find the truth, so he asked to spend a night in the supposedly haunted room. However, he believed the 'haunting' was merely local smugglers using Raynham Hall as their home base, and they wanted to keep people away from their goods.

Florence Marryat said his father stayed in the room that had the portrait of the apparition. By comparing the ghost to this portrait, people realized it was Lady Dorothy who was haunting them. She was most often seen in this room, and it was possibly the room in which she took her last breath. Marryat slept in that room each night, with a revolver stashed beneath his pillow. For the first two days, there were no signs of anything paranormal. On the third night, though, two young men called on him to help authenticate a gun that was arriving from London that day. As he left the room, he took his revolver, joking that it was for safety, "In case we meet the Brown Lady."

Dressed in nothing but shirt and trousers—indecent attire for that era—Marryat accompanied the men down the hall. Initially, they glimpsed a lamp coming towards them. The two young men with him figured it was probably one of the mansion's ladies on her way to visit the nursery. The men crept away from the woman, mainly because of Marryat's immodest clothing.

As they watched, Marryat was stunned to realize she was wearing the infamous brown brocade gown, and she was none other than the Brown Lady. Pulling out his revolver, and demand the truth when she stopped at the door behind which he was hiding. Marryat claimed that she lifted the lamp she was carrying to highlight her sunken features and then grinned at him in a malicious and diabolical manner.

An ordinary man might have frozen in such a situation. But Marryat yanked his revolver hard and discharged the bullet right into her face. It passed right through her and lodged itself in the wall as the Brown Lady vanished. Marryat returned home and never again attempted to return to Raynham Hall to seek the Brown Lady.

The next reported sighting of Lady Dorothy happened in 1926, which the then Lady Townshend recorded. Her son and his friend had been playing on the staircase together. When they felt an unusual chill and caught sight of the ghost, it wasn't long before they realized she was the same woman in the portrait, and they concluded it was the Brown Lady.

The most infamous sighting of the Brown Lady happened in 1936, when she was captured on film and nationalized in *Country Life* magazine, catapulting her and Raynham Hall to fame. On September 19, 1936, a London photographer named Captain Hubert Provand came to Raynham Hall with his assistant, Indre Shira. They both worked for *Country Life* magazine, and wanted to take pictures of the manor for an article. They were also intrigued by the mansion's history and ghastly legend. Their photograph was one of the first ghost pictures ever captured, and this garnered much attention.

They had just taken a picture of the manor's main staircase when Shira caught sight of the veiled form floating down the stairs. Shira pressed down on the trigger and captured the image, but it was not until they developed the picture that they realized they caught the Brown Lady on camera. The photograph and their story was published in *Country Life*, making them famous almost overnight.

Noted paranormal investigator Harry Price interviewed them. He claimed their story was legitimate, given that they did not even realize they were capturing a ghost on camera. The negative was verified as not being tampered with and found to be authentic. Logic dictates that the truth is what's left when one eliminates all other possibilities, no matter how bizarre or unbelievable it is. And it's thought that the Brown Lady exists, and two amateur photographers captured her on film.

Over the years, various people have studied the photograph and argued the truth behind it. Modern science has examined the picture time and again, and each time, results have been inconclusive. There is a claim that the image could be an accidental double exposure or that light got inside of the camera by mistake, or even that Shira and Provand faked the photograph. Also, if any of these theories were true, it only proves that the *picture* is a fake, not that the Brown Lady herself is.

After the picture was published, sightings of the Brown Lady haunting the rooms and staircase continued, although they have dwindled through the years. The late Marchioness of Townsend reported having seen her several times in the late 1960s, and many of the housekeeping staff talk about the cold drafts and lights typical of haunting within the manor.

Many believe that she still lingers in the hallowed halls, waiting for a release from her prison. Such a tragedy, trapped by her own family and left to die, going insane, all this anger and hate inside her with no closure. She still roams the manor, haunted by what happened centuries ago, waiting for the day when, once and for all, she will be able to leave Raynham Hall.

CHAPTER 3:
EMAILS FROM THE OTHER SIDE

A UNIQUE AND RELATIVELY RECENT INCIDENT, Jack Froese's story is told through personal accounts of those touched by it. This story can be one of horror, as well as joy, depending on how you cope with and view the death of someone close to you. Some may find it deeply unsettling or horrifying, while others find solace in the experience if they have lost someone dear to them. Either way, everybody will agree that the freak occurrence described by Froese's friends and family is incredibly strange.

In the words of his loved ones, Jack Froese was a kind, sensitive, and a well-liked man living in Dunmore, Pennsylvania. Unfortunately, he passed away at the young age of thirty-two in June of 2011 from complications of cardiac arrhythmia. His death was sudden and shocked those around him, leaving them grieving. He survived by his mother, Patty Froese, his longtime friend, Tim Hart, and his cousin, Jimmy McGraw, whom he was close to.

Jack's friends and family began to accept the loss and cope with it as best as possible, moving on with their lives and coming to terms with life without him. This way of dealing with the death would have been a familiar story of human loss, grief, and letting go of someone special had it not been for the bizarre events that began to occur a few months after Jack's death.

In November of 2011, Tim Hart and Jimmy McGraw were stunned to receive separate emails from their deceased friend's email account. The messages were rather personal and referred to some of the final conversations and situations they found themselves in with Jack, not long before his untimely death. These unique details infused the emails with an extraordinary level of credibility and authenticity, making it exceedingly difficult for his friends to brush them off as a big prank by someone who had hacked into Jack's account.

Both Tim Hart and Jimmy McGraw also believe, as they have stated in an interview given to the BBC, that nobody could have possibly known the password for Jack's email account. So a case of hacking was doubtful. Both Hart and McGraw discussed and showed the contents of the emails they received from the deceased in the BBC's TV interview.

The message that Hart received stood out in his email inbox, not only because of the deceased sender, but also due to its eerie subject title, which concisely stated, "I'm watching." When Tim Hart first saw this message, he remembered he turned white as a sheet with utter disbelief. After the initial shock faded, and he opened the email. He was greeted by the familiar, light-hearted tone in the email message, characteristic of the Jack Froese he knew and loved. This message from "Jack" read, "Did you hear me? I'm at your house. Clean your f***ing attic!"

These messages were especially shocking to Tim, since not long before his friend's death, Jack joked on how Tim's attic desperately needed cleaned. They had a private conversation, and Hart says that nobody else knew about it, nor would even think of saying such a thing in an email. He was unsure what to make of the message, but he still replied to it, hoping to elicit a response from beyond the grave. Unfortunately, no answer that we know of ever came back.

Likewise, the email sent to Jimmy McGraw pertained to his matters as well, but this time, regarding issues that occurred after Jack's death. McGraw explains in the interview that he broke his ankle about a week before he received an email in November 2011, on his way to work. In the message McGraw received, "Jack" asked how he was doing and told him that he knew Jimmy would sustain the injury, and had tried to warn him. "Jack" then said Jim ought to be careful, made a couple of short personal remarks, and ended with his name as a signature. McGraw noted that he saw only a couple of friends and a few family members while he was recovering following his injury.

Despite the initial bewilderment brought about by the eerily personal emails from their departed friend, the people Jack left behind soon came to terms with what happened. But, of course, it remains unclear whether this bizarre correspondence was a distasteful, cruel prank or actual communication with the deceased Jack Froese from the realm beyond our own. Of course, many people would probably be very disturbed if they received a message or a perceived sign from their dead loved ones, but this wasn't the case with the folks Jack left behind.

Jack Froese's mother, Patty, told the interviewers that the emails delighted some people, while they disturbed others. However, she accepted them with an open heart and told Jack's loved ones that the messages were a gift from him and that they should take them as such. She gave little thought to whether they were just a cruel prank. Instead, she was grateful because these mysterious emails got people to keep talking again about her son and kept his memory alive.

Hart and McGraw were similarly minded on the matter. Hart said he didn't care if it was a prank. Hart wholeheartedly accepted the advice from Jack's mother. Saying he would take this mystery the way he wanted to, but accepting it as a good thing in the end. McGraw had similar feelings, and described how hard his cousin's sudden departure hit him, explaining he viewed the emails as Jack's attempts to help him feel better and move on. He concluded he liked the fact that he received the mysterious and unexplained email.

Dealing with death and loss is a personal and subjective experience we must go through it our own way. This story has a profound effect on many since it can be a personal experience. It's possible someone they knew sent these emails. Who would ever think of pulling such a nasty joke on their friends? But then again, we don't know if they were also somehow sent by Jack

Froese from beyond the grave to tease his dear loved ones for one last time. Either way, Jack's inner circle got something heartfelt out of the whole experience and found a sort of closure in the mysterious messages, helping them to move on. How would you have felt receiving such an unexplained and eerie message from the realm of the unknown?

CHAPTER 4:
TO RAISE THE DEVIL

NUMEROUS GHOST STORIES ARE ABOUT SIGHTINGS OF SINGLE APPARITIONS, whose tales begin with some horrible or traumatic event resulting in a tragic end—souls confined to the location where the vile crimes took place. But when a site is subject to the constant visitation of more than a single spirit, then that story would indeed be a horrifying haunting.

Asylums have always been sites of hauntings and for a good reason. During earlier times, these places were treated as graveyards for the mentally ill. Then, during the pre-dawn of modern medicine and enlightened psychology interpretations, the insane and mentally disturbed were discarded by their families and sent to faraway institutions. The doctors at these institutions had a freehand with performing horrific experiments on these patients, all in the dubious name of science. It is little wonder the ghosts of the hundreds of disturbed innocents who were tortured and killed there haunt many of these old asylums.

Of these many institutions, the Taunton State Hospital in Massachusetts was one of the most horrific places where the Devil himself was said to have walked through the halls. The Hospital opened in 1854, called then the State Lunatic Hospital in Taunton, and served as the second state asylum. Ironically, it was built per the specifications of Dr. Thomas Kirkbride, who advocated treating all mentally ill patients with care and compassion. They could be best advised through positivity and good feelings, not by shunning them or fearing them, as most people were inclined to do.

The hospital's building followed his designs, including a large campus for patients to wander with recreation rooms and comfortable bedrooms. The patients were supposed to have sunlight, fresh air, good food, and plenty of space to move around. It had bridge ways to keep the wards connected to the hospital's infirmary wing. The hospital was aesthetically beautiful and quite pleasing to the eye.

However, the outer beauty could not hide the inner ugliness that was taking place in its hallowed halls. Its history is bloody, murderous, and painful. Thousands of patients were tortured, and over the years, several staff members have reported stories of being victims themselves of some paranormal phenomenon.

Taunton itself hosted several infamous people within its walls. Thomas Hubbard Sumner, the inventor of the Sumner Line, was one such patient who spent his last days in this hospital.

Convicted serial killer Jane Toppan was also sentenced to life here, and her story is quite a chilling tale. Toppan, who lost her mother when she was just a child, was raised by her father, an alcoholic and eccentric madman nicknamed 'Kelley the Crack.' He left his two daughters at the Boston Female Asylum and vanished. Jane, adopted as the servant of the well-to-do Toppan family, took their last name.

As she grew up and trained to be a nurse, she started using her patients as her guinea pigs, dosing them with various drugs such as morphine and atropine. She claimed that the sight of patients close to death aroused her sexually. She would dose them, get into bed with them, and hold them close as they passed away. She later moved back to her hometown, where she killed her foster sister and attempted to seduce her widowed brother-in-law after the gruesome act. With her foster sister dead, she tried to convince her sister's husband that she loved him by poisoning him, only to nurse him back to health. She also poisoned herself to gain sympathy from him. These attempts to get her brother-in-law's attention did not work, and he sent her away. Investigations of her previous murders led to her arrest, where she confessed to having killed over thirty people. They sentenced Jane to life at the Taunton State Asylum. Her ghost, it is said, still haunts the halls, drawing people closer to death and holding them tight as they pass into the void.

Madness, violence, and murder ran rampant within the halls of Taunton. Yet, while many patients housed within the facility were genuinely disturbed, what was far more frightening were the secret activities of the doctors and staff members themselves at Taunton.

According to local legend, Taunton was the site of cult activity and devil worship. There were rumors of patients routinely being sacrificed to Satan and other demons. Staff members allegedly brought the most helpless patients down to the basement to be offered to the dark lord as sacrificial lambs. After having heard the rumors, some patients refused to be brought down to the basement. Because of this, they lost their outdoor privileges.

What exactly happened in the basement? We can only speculate. Many staff members report the basement remains icy cold even in the middle of summer, and numerous cold spots move throughout the entire hospital. Even today, strange markings in blood cover the basement walls where these rumored murder rituals took place. Possibly hundreds of lost souls are still trapped within these haunted corridors, trying to reach out in the only way they know-how.

One staff member decided he would like to see the truth for himself. As he walked down the length of the stairs, he stopped on the final step, unable to move further. Rooted to the spot, he described what could only be a paranormal experience. As he closed his eyes, he felt every single case of torture and pain that each of the tormented souls trapped within the hospital went through. He raced back upstairs and resigned from his job that very day. Even now, he has trouble explaining what he saw and went through and remains traumatized by his experience.

The hospital isn't the only thing that haunts the people of Massachusetts. The woods surrounding it are just as terrifying. Allegedly, satanic rituals have taken place there as well. People have reported hearing the groaning moans, desperate cries, and frantic calls for help at night. Banging noises are a daily occurrence, as are flashing lights and strange, cold drafts.

Some of the latter staff reported seeing a man in white walking around the third-floor corridors. He flickers in and out of visibility, becoming physical and then vanishing, coming and going as he wishes. Sometimes, he is simply a shadow that crawls across the wall in a slow, terrifying manner, as though looking for something. Other times, he becomes a solid figure, striding across the hallway in a rage. The apparition is always a male, but no one has ever clearly seen his face. Residents have reported that he stands in the corner of their rooms and watches them silently. Switch on the lights, and he vanishes, his face always hidden in the shadows.

Could he be one of the many victims who was tortured and killed at Taunton? Or is he the Devil himself, waiting to ensnare unsuspecting victims? Did the doctors, through their heinous acts of brutality and murder, raise Satan himself? Is the victim or perpetrator? Or perhaps even both? We can only speculate.

The cemetery is also quite a haunting site. One resident reports a chilling story. A patient escaped the halls of Taunton. He ran out of the facility but tired quickly and unable to run any further, he waited the night out in the graveyard. It seemed to be a good idea because no one would think of looking for him within the grounds of the hospital itself.

As he crouched near a tombstone, he felt the icy grip of a hand holding his shoulder tight enough to bruise it. Thinking someone captured him, he threw his arms up, turning around to face his captor, only to see that there was *no one* behind him. A second later, a whisper murmured into his ear, "Leave." It repeated itself again and again. Finally, panicked and terrified, the man ran back into the hospital, where he spent the rest of his days.

Did both the spectral hand and the disembodied voice belong to a ghost attempting to warn him to escape the halls of Taunton? Or was it the Devil himself, trying to frighten the man into staying? One can only wonder.

Doors slam, lights flash, and icy chills occur within the rooms of Taunton. The shadows dance, but not pleasantly. The silhouettes speak of unimaginable horror, of the hundreds of innocents whose bloodshed to bring the Devil to life within the walls of Taunton. It is not surprising that this has become one of the most haunted places in the United States of America.

Taunton State Hospital, supposedly a sanctuary for the mentally disturbed where they might find peace of mind and solace of spirit, became something else. The doctors, meant to be their caretakers, turned into their captors as they used them as sacrificial lambs for slaughter, cutting into them and offering them up as bait for their satanic rituals.

Whether it was psychotic criminals like Jane Toppan or the innocent victims whose families shipped them off to Taunton, thousands of trapped souls within the halls, to this day, their souls have not found a way out of the mental institution. Instead, they remain imprisoned, long after their bodies have died and rot under the ground.

CHAPTER 5:
THE PECULIAR CASE OF JULIA

THERE IS RARELY A CASE OF POSSESSION, HAUNTING, GHOST SIGHTING, or anything else relating to the paranormal scientists ever notice. And if they do care to comment on the stories and give their opinions, they are almost entirely skeptical and even ridicule the idea. After all, if anybody were to debunk a particular paranormal event, it is usually scientists. It is their job to seek material evidence that can be put to the test, proving a theory beyond any doubt, and basing their understanding of reality on which can be observed, measured, tested, and verified.

However, occasionally something unusual appears which the scientific community takes notices of, investigates, and documents. Such is the story of Dr. Richard Gallagher, a board-certified psychiatrist and a professor of clinical psychiatry at the

New York Medical College. In 2008, Dr. Gallagher spoke of a particular case regarding a woman referred to only as "Julia", although her real identity remains confidential. He brought forth the situation through an article he published in the New Oxford Review. He called what was happening to Julia, a "contemporary, clear-cut case of demonic possession." Furthermore, the doctor — himself a believer in the phenomenon — said that this case would prove very convincing to even the firmest of skeptics.

What appeared to be another instance of a highly disturbed, tormented soul soon seemed like much more than that. However, according to the doctor's testimony, as well as those of quite a few other people involved, the affliction that struck Julia's mind and soul may not have been of this dimension. The witnesses to some of her demonic episodes included priests, assistants, deacons, nuns, and psychiatrists. Believe it or not, all these people were present to see the extraordinary paranormal occurrences in some of Julia's worst episodes, including levitation.

Everything points to Julia consulting with priests and Dr. Gallagher of her own volition. Wishing to undergo a Roman Catholic exorcism, Julia sought the assistance of a priest. Simultaneously, in his capacity as a psychiatric professional, Gallagher was called in to rule out the possibility of mental illness. The doctor had no idea what was to come.

According to what little information Gallagher disclosed about her, Julia was a middle-aged, employed, white American. Most importantly, she was bright, showed no signs of mental illness, and was normally reasonable. She had been a Catholic for a time, but she subsequently went down a different path.

The woman had a dark, lengthy history of involvement with Satanist groups, with whom she had participated in many satanic rituals. Over time, she felt that a demon, or even Satan himself, might have possessed her as her life deteriorated rapidly on all fronts. She was sure of this by the time Gallagher and the rest of the team got involved.

In Gallagher's own words, the exorcising of Julia's supposed demons commenced with a ritual in June, on an expectedly warm day. The doctor further explained that the room where the exorcism was about to be carried out was unnaturally cold, despite the rising temperatures outside. However, the room grew warm beyond comfort as the exorcism was well underway. The intensity of the exorcism was said to give off immense heat, which almost forced everybody out.

At the beginning of the exorcism, things were relatively quiet as Julia appeared to drift away into a serene trance. Gallagher explained Julia would often go into all kinds of trances . Although dislodgment from reality is common among many mentally ill individuals, Julia's particular episode occurred in strange aspects. Her voice would change rapidly and oscillate between high and low pitches, sometimes sounding rather deep and intimidating. The voices seemed very unnatural and foreign to the Julia they knew when she wasn't experiencing these states. The alleged demons would hurl insults and threats through her, and Julia referred to herself in the third person. It seemed evident the voices appeared to come from a source separate from Julia's person. The voices would say that Julia belonged to them, and they would warn the team to leave her alone and give up, or they would regret it. In between the insults and the taunts, all those present observed that she made bizarre screeches, roars, and monstrous growls unbecoming of any human being. As expected, Julia had no recollection of what she was saying and doing after she would snap back to reality.

Indeed, one could have suggested this was somewhat like a multiple personality disorder, a life-crippling mental illness that plagues quite a few people. However, being a seasoned psychiatrist, would have been the first to make such a diagnosis, ruling this theory out. This exorcism became even more evident as her verbal expressions soon took quite a dizzying turn for the paranormal.

The inhuman fits of rage and the overall viciousness of these demonic outbursts were the least of the coming terrors. Julia randomly spoke in languages such as Spanish and Latin—languages which she didn't speak a word of otherwise. It was during these freakish episodes that Julia, or whatever entity had taken hold of her, exhibited psychic abilities as well. She made comments regarding the personal information and details of the lives of those present, although she had no way of knowing these things. Doctor Gallagher mentioned a few specific instances of this phenomenon.

She appeared to have insight into the team's family life, including deaths, tragedies, illness, and other deeply personal matters. For example, one of the team members was shocked to hear Julia describing the life and health of a relative and how he died. Julia correctly "guessed" that the relative had died of cancer and, more impressively, she also stated what type of cancer it was.

Similarly, she was aware that another team member's household cats had a bloody, ferocious fight among themselves the night before. Of course, she'd never seen the team member's house nor the cats. There was no way of knowing this person even *had* cats. Yet, she teased the team member with comments on how brutal the cats were to each other. When he returned to his home in a completely different city the next day, he confirmed the event she described. He didn't know his cats to fight like that before.

You'd be wrong to think that Dr. Gallagher's account stops here. Many of Julia's attacks and demonic outbursts were physical, not just verbal and psychological. Namely, the doctor described near-superhuman strength, very unbecoming of an average-size, female human. Keeping her restrained was an incredibly difficult task, and several people were hardly enough to keep her down. Things rose to a whole new level of bizarre with the doctor's description of the horror that came next. He said that everyone in the team was terrified a Julia levitated a foot above the floor. In defiance of the most fundamental laws of nature, she remained in this mind-boggling state for around half an hour.

Gallagher also described Julia, or the force within her, as having telekinetic abilities. The objects in the room would fly out of place and be tossed around entirely on their own. Books and other things were launched from their shelves, rendering the situation quite dangerous for the team in the room.

Ending in finally cleansing Julia, the team concluded that the exorcism had most likely been successful. Though Gallagher had his doubts, we'll probably never know if the alleged demon expelled from the woman, if it decided to lie dormant as a trick to fool the exorcists, or if there is some other explanation for her behavior. One might assume that the rite was successful.

Based on similar stories in pop culture films, one might expect the demon could be triggered into activity by religious stimulus in the future. Dr. Gallagher has released very few personal details about his subject, and we don't know if he kept in touch with her after the fact. Thus, Julia's subsequent fate remains a mystery.

This account of demonic possession is incredibly straightforward. It shocks both logic and reason. Movies and books have tapped into these stories as subject matter, giving them a strange appreciation. However, stories like these can be easy ammunition for the skeptics when the source is questionable. Certain people are deemed unstable, prone to fantasies, and have minimal credibility. But, when a man with such high standing and top qualifications such as Dr. Gallagher writes a paper, outlining this kind of finding, in such a direct and transparent way. It gives the story an uncanny resonance.

Of course, that's not to say he's perfect and incapable of lying and creating a hoax. But his reputation would be at stake. The source of information is always one of the main factors skeptics examine when looking at a paranormal story. Using it to determine the potential validity of the encounter–and it should be no different in this instance as well.

CHAPTER 6:
THE ROOSEVELT HOTEL

THE FAME OF THE ROOSEVELT HOTEL IS UNPARALLELED. The Hollywood monolith first stood as a glamorous structure in 1927, right in the thick of Los Angeles. As such, it was a hotspot of the Hollywood elite, and its Blossom Ballroom was the first host of the Academy Awards. From then, it was a venue for more notable ceremonies like the Golden Raspberry Awards and was a scene for popular films such as Bruce Willis's Sunset.

Currently, it is a historic and cultural monument of the City of Angels, and a luxury hotel to opulent travelers. But frighteningly, the hotel has—for reasons to be told later—long been rumored to be connected to the supernatural. The rumors range from furtive, familiar figures seen from the corner of an eye to the spine-chilling sounds supposedly not heard. As these rumors grew into whispered stories veiled in half-truths and sensations, they persisted to be retold endlessly, even up to this moment.

As the oldest running hotel in Los Angeles, the historic Roosevelt Hotel has a decorated past and star-studded chronicle. A retreat for Hollywood celebrities, the hotel was named after US President Theodore Roosevelt when it opened in 1927. It was financed by movie mogul Louis Mayer and famous American stars Mary Pickford and Douglas Fairbanks Jr., among others. It was a colossal architectural achievement for its time, as it boasted of three hundred rooms and suites while serving as an iconic setting for various films and movies.

In 1929, its Blossom Ballroom hosted the first Academy Awards. The event was a private dinner celebrating the best movies of 1927 and 1928. 270 guests, each with an attendance ticket valued at five dollars, packed the room. They were the only witnesses of the fifteen golden statuettes awarded in only fifteen minutes.

But starting in the mid 1950s, the hotel's status declined until it was bought by the Radissons in the 1980s. There were many restorations and renovations since then. It was a classy Spanish-style interior LA spot along the Hollywood Walk of Fame and across the street from the TCL Chinese Theatre.

Through the years, the Roosevelt Hotel received the likes of Charlie Chaplin, Clark Gable, and Carole Lombard. One of its fixtures was a youthful Norma Jeane Mortenson. The young model and actress, popularly known as Marilyn Monroe, did her first photoshoot at the hotel's poolside. As her modelling and acting career took off, she lived in Roosevelt's room 229 for the better part of her two years. The 750 square foot room is now immortalized as the Marilyn Suite.

Over time, there have been rumors of hauntings in the hotel. Some involved stars like Montgomery Clift, Errol Flynn, and Norma Jeane herself. Being home to Hollywood's household names for almost its entire existence, it should come as no surprise to hear it may be host to ghostly sightings of the famous.

The Roosevelt Hotel was a landmark for Norma Jeane Mortenson's fans, as it was the actress's home for two years just as her career was taking off. Known to most as Marilyn Monroe, the American star stayed at the Cabana-styled room 229 and had her first model photoshoot at the hotel's famed Tropicana Pool. The Roosevelt was such a significant venue during Norma's career and life that the blonde bombshell continues to saunter around the hotel even after her passing in 1962.

In 1986, a cleaning woman swore she saw Marilyn. One day, while she was sweeping room 229, she said the suite's mirror reflected the recognizable, beautiful blonde features of Marilyn Monroe. But as she turned back to face the figure, there was nothing there but the quiet walls and an eerie silence. Many others claimed to have a similar experience, and eventually the full-length glass was transferred to the hotel lobby. However, it did not stop the continuing apparitions of the blonde ghost.

This attracted people from all over and turned the 750 square foot cabana suite into a destination for those who wished to have a chance encounter with the showbiz spirit. One of them was a young woman from California. Fresh out of college in 2011, she gifted herself a stay in the infamous room. From the first moment she walked in, she said she felt a strange presence and power emanating from the space. And in that space she would see Mariyln Monroe's apparition on occasions when whe would lease expect it. She still remembers the haunting sensation until now, she says.

Another creepy account came in 2018, when a young woman and her best friend stayed the night at the Roosevelt Monroe Room, hoping to have a classy experience in the well-known hotel landmark. On that evening, as she slowly combed her hair after a chilly bath, she says she turned to see Marilyn's face in her best friend's ash-blond strands. She screamed at the sight of it. Yet after a blink and a gasp, the ghost of the actress vanished. She recalls the experience as being, "Strange, shocking, and definitely scary."

These are not the only stories told about the spiritual sighting of Marilyn Monroe in the Roosevelt hotel. Tales of Norma Jeane's ghostly presence abound, and many ask why she still resides in the Hollywood landmark, even after death. Could it be that Norma went back to the place where she had a breakthrough in her Hollywood vocation, wishing to relive the experience and be around the hotel she loved the most? Or is her residual energy and unconscious spiritual emotions forever attached to the place? We may never know, unless she tells you personally during your own stay in the Marilyn suite of the Roosevelt.

Marilyn Monroe, however, is not the only celebrity ghost haunting the hotel. Edward Montgomery Clift is one other. The actor lived at the Roosevelt for three months while he was filming the 1953 movie, *From Here to Eternity*. During his stay in room 928, he rehearsed his lines seriously and took breaks playing his trumpet. He had a staggered career, and was allegedly picky with the roles given to him. Sadly, a devastating car accident in 1956 ruined his face. Though there were no pictures of Montgomery Clift's broken features, he never really recovered from it and his career went to a slow but sure decline. Still, many fondly remember an immaculate expression to an earnest face, while some recall him as a rebel and a mischievous individual.

This mischievousness is still felt by guests of the Roosevelt, and accounts of this are numerous. Several guests claim vexation from their shoulders being tapped by Clift's ghostly hands. A couple, for example, say they stayed in Edward Montgomery's old room and immediately had a ghastly occurence.

One night, the wife was awakened by a gentle tap from her husband and was about to return the good night gesture. But when she turned over, she found he was so deeply asleep that the tap could not have come from him. Gasping in horror, she rolled back over, closed her eyes, and hoped to wake up to find it was all her imagination. However, she remembered it so clearly the next morning she insisted that it must have been Clift's hands that touched her shoulder.

People in neighboring rooms have professed these same hands play the trumpet on various occasions. They insist it must be Clift because their noise complaints were met by deaf ears by the staff, who disclosed that no guests were staying in the room at that time.

Other visitors swear to have seen Edward Montgomery's spirit pacing the hotel's hallways while practicing old lines on aged scripts. And cleaning ladies of the Roosevelt once saw the actor's apparition on the ninth floor, and an unsettling feeling crept by them when a spectral wind breezed along their backs when they were cleaning 928.

A more recent encounter with the Hollywood ghost came from a psychic who stayed in the room. He claims that he felt anger, tragedy, and brokenness; even along the corridors near the room and the stairs nearby. He said feeling was so intense that for a long moment the next morning, he could not move or get up from the bed. He said it felt like the ghost of Montgomery Clift on top of him. He struggled and eventually pushed away the spirit before hurrying from the room. As he left, right before he closed the door, he claims to have seen the black stare of the Clift spirit.

Despite these stories being passed, read, and heard by many of Roosevelt hotel's patrons and would-be guests, many still seek the thrill of an encounter with the dark apparition. Others simply wish to stay in a room once occupied by a celebrated Hollywood actor whose high cheekbones, set jaw, and firm stare captured the imagination of 50's popular culture before fading away until he died in 1966.

The ghost stories do not stop here for the historic, yet ill-famed Roosevelt. It is not just celebrity icons who in lived there and may be haunting it. In 2005, a major renovation of the place was completed, and the spirits seemed to approve of the new look and enjoyed their afterlife at the better residences of the

Hollywood hotel. There were many experiences that bore witness to ghosts of less known, wraithlike characters or were recipients of messages from unknown sources.

Employees at the front desk claim on occasion to get calls from supposedly vacant rooms, and when they investigated one such occurence, claim to have heard giggles and chuckles. Surprised to hear sounds from the other side of the door, they unlocked it, turned the knob, and opened to an empty space. There was no one there. Similar stories recall sounds of classic typewriters in unoccupied rooms. "It was crazy," said one of the witnesses who heard noises in places where there should have been no people present.

Another guest who booked a spirit-inhabited room for two told of moving curtains in the shower. As she hurriedly stepped out of the bath, she screamed and swore to her friend that she felt a ghost in the bathroom.

The spine-chilling experience scared both of them enough to go to another hotel for the night. They were sure they would not forget the encounter for many nights thereafter, and people like them continue to pour accounts of their chilling experiences at the Roosevelt Hotel. Aside from this, further eerie, paranormal experiences include weird electric malfunctions, strange disconnection of cell phone receptions, breaking elevators, and swimming spirits at the Tropicana Pool.

Guards purportedly hear splashes of water in the swimming pool while guests should be in their beds, fast asleep. One of them went to the water and reported the sounds to his colleague while looking and waving at the security camera by the poolside.

The colleague checked the flashing video and said he saw the gesturing hand behind a ghost's transparent head. Upon reviewing the video, the guards saw nothing except the first guard.

The famous Blossom Ballroom also has had its share of creepy and ghoulish occurrences. A tuxedo-dressed male persona was said to be seen roaming around the dance hall, exuding a feeling of anxiety. Though his identity is unknown, some say he was in attendance during the first Academy Awards and was a nominee of one of the fifteen golden statuettes. Perhaps in his disappointment of not having won the gold prize, he continues to linger and cannot let go of the significant ceremony just yet.

Another male ghost shares the same attachment. Visitors of the Roosevelt heard piano chords during their stroll on the mezzanine. When they looked over the balcony, they saw a smokey apparition of a man in a white suit who quickly disappeared with a passing wind, prompting the onlookers to question the truth of what they had seen. Was it real, or just their minds playing tricks on them? Attempts to take footage of such spiritual sightings have been foiled by unexplainable voltaic failures that skeptics claim to be evidence of a hoax.

What was not professedly a hoax was the entity of a five-year-old girl. People popularly name her Caroline. She was frequently seen at the hotel's main lobby, and resembled a real, living child. Walking around and strolling past patrons in jeans and jacket, she asked for her mother and father from the clientele.

The story behind the young ghost, who has also been spotted skipping and singing, is that she and her brother drowned in the pool while their father was out running errands. This leads some to believe that the brother also haunts the hotel. A boy who may be him has been frequently seen in the library, near payphones, and in jacuzzies with Caroline. They seem to delight in teasing the Roosevelt staff, because when they come to investigate these sightings, they quickly vanished then returned soon after, leading to an unending cycle of a ghostly game of tag.

It is interesting that where these children came from is unknown. Having no history, it is a mystery why these child ghosts roam the floors of the Roosevelt. Psychics and paranormal experts suggest they could not move on because they are still waiting for their parents. Though this may be their reason for not passing on to the next life, they seem to enjoy the extravagance of the grand hotel.

Other restless spirits stay with other intentions.

"A lot of spirits stick around for unfinished business," declared Laurie Jacobson, author of the book *Hollywood Haunted*. Marilyn Monroe attempts to find the quietude of an earlier part in her life and career, before unwanted decisions, turns, and twists led to her death. Edward Montgomery Clift is believed to be trapped, unable to find the peace he sought in his life, and still seeking it in the hotel. Caroline and her brother are searching for their parents, asking unknowing visitors about their whereabouts. Other former residents like Carol Lumbard, Errol Flynn, Carmen Miranda, Humphrey Bogart, and Betty Grable have strong emotions that tie them to the Roosevelt.

Their rumored appearances to guests and employees make the Roosevelt arguably the most haunted hotel in Los Angeles, backed by countless anecdotes and testimonies from witnesses. These narratives of haunts tell of ghosts grumbling for attention. Many fans of the time-passed celebrities and adrenaline junkies have taken an immense interest in visiting the prodigious, spirit-frequented structure.

Individuals who claim to have been successful hunt say the spirits of the former residents truly still reside in their old rooms. Some of these people were filled with fright. Others admired the company of once well-known showbiz stars.

But, remains no scientific proof of their existence. This has not diminished the collective enthusiasm around the hotel. According to a 2009 survey by YouGovAmerica, 45 percent of Americans believes in the paranormal.

A more recent survey in 2019 by Chapman University found that 19 percent of the US population believe themselves to have seen or encountered the paranormal; a number of them coming from the Roosevelt Hotel.

John Tenney, who considers himself a paranormal expert and one-time host of the television show *Ghost Stalkers*, does not doubt that a chunk of these cases is explainable and the noises people have heard are no more than the din of popping bricks and expanding wood. "People are just not used to the sounds they should've been hearing in the morning since most of them are out," he says. However, visitors of the Roosevelt Hotel insisted on the realness of the voices.

One occupant says she heard an argument between a couple from a neighboring room, whose heated exchange she was not able to make out. When she complained about it to the hotel staff, they swore there was no one there. Other guests attested they heard this kind of talk and felt cold, human-like touches on different occasions. These may have come from the same vanished couple, or a totally different presence.

Other experiences tell of small objects—including keys, cards, coins, and cash—moving to strange places, along with the reappearance of formerly lost items such as cameras and cell phones. The fearless travelers who have spent the night in the Roosevelt have described the sense of being watched by an unknown entity and icy breath breathing on their necks.

If their persistent contact becomes too much, one can always head downstairs for the music and dance at the cool and classy Blossom Ballroom, but one must not be surprised if it is a ghost-only party. Troubling as it may be, Mr. Tenney, the *Ghost Stalkers* host, offers some words of wisdom to the troubled haunted. "Don't panic. Observe and take notes. You may soon find logic finding your fears to be false." But what if the encounter manifests truth and reality then confounds, disconcerts, troubles, rattles, and horrifies? Mr. Tenny also offers this: "The ghost you have been seeing haunting the place has been there before you even realized it was there. You are the one who might have changed, your eyes wide open to the weirder and a stranger truth of an odder world."

Always accompanied by the night, the Roosevelt Hotel ghost stories always occupy the edges of human perception. They may involve insidious images of figures seen from the corner of an eye or spooky sounds where there should be none, such as loud knocks on the door without announcements. They can be remembered or exotic scents. Or just a strange feeling, as if there is someone nearby. Sometimes they are accompanied by the eclipsing of the moon or complete lack thereof. These ghost stories the Roosevelt Hotel cannot seem to get rid of, or is not allowed to.

Do you believe in ghosts? Since ancient times, many people have believed in them. Some still believe spirits dwell among the living. It is likely the most popular paranormal belief that exists. Yet, among all the stories and tales surrounding it, there is no scientific evidence of its reality. But there are people who make a living trying to answer the question. They use night-vision and thermal imaging technology that they claim can identify spirits. Others use audio-recording equipment that supposedly can record the sounds they make.

Lisa, of Contact Research Investigation Specialists — or CRIS, claims to have recorded Marilyn Monroe's voice in suite 229 at the Roosevelt Hotel. She conducted a paranormal investigation with para-psychologist Doctor Berry Taft. Both claim to have heard a cry for help in the audio file.

While these types of technology have their uses to ghost hunters, some choose the traditional method of communicating with the dead–using Ouija boards and planchettes. Some even state to have a sixth sense. Psychic Peter James is one of them. He claims to have physically seen Marilyn Monroe with his gift, and argues the actress is looking for peace, thus unable to move on to the afterlife.

Another claim of his is contact with Montgomery Clift in room 928, where he was paralyzed by his spirit, but eventually able to break free from his ghostly hold. From the experience, he concluded that the actor was restless, stuck, and unable to find the solitude he is looking for at the Roosevelt. He also found a cold spot in the Blossom Ballroom that he called a "tubular shaft", a doorway used by visiting souls who cannot seem to retreat to where they are supposed to be after their passing.

Other pathways may take on different forms, and may be used to communicate to passing life. The ghosts may look like how they did when they were alive. Other times, they are just a flicker of light, or a numb or sharp sensation. Some ghosts are not seen, but heard–a knock, a closing door, a turning knob, a low moan, or a sad cry.

But when it comes to ghosts, it is usually a conflict of science versus the stories. Both on opposite sides of the coin. But if something has not been scientifically proven, does it make it any less real?

In the end, the evidence of these spectral entities being true is no better at the present than it was decades ago. Reasons for this can all boil down to two causes. One, ghosts do not exist and reports of them can be explained by psychology, misperceptions, and hoaxes. The second is that they are real,but the mindset, tools, and equipment to gather meaningful evidence of their existence are not yet available.

Ultimately, even if the vindications make sense, one believes what one wants to believe. It helps some to consider a world beyond the physical realm. So, wherever you land on this issue, you should consider booking a room at the famous Roosevelt Hotel. And hope that the ghost you meet from the Hollywood elite is in a good mood.

CHAPTER 7:
ROBERT THE DOLL

EVEN IF YOU'VE NEVER HEARD OF ROBERT THE DOLL, odds are you've heard of the famous Chucky doll from *Child's Play*. In the 1988 film, a young boy's mother giving him a sinister children's toy as a gift. As time goes on, the child realizes that this new doll is anything but what he expected. Instead, Chucky reveals himself as a living toy that commits evil acts at every chance he gets.

Unfortunately, most people don't know that parts of Chucky's story are based on a real doll. The terrifying legacy of Robert the Doll is said to be possessed by a malicious and vengeful spirit. But don't let his innocent appearance deceive you, as his disturbing story has earned its rank as one of the eeriest dolls in the world.

In 1906 a young boy named Robert Eugene Otto received a doll from his grandparents. The doll was three feet tall, dressed in a sailor's outfit, and holding a small lion by his side. The boy joyfully took the doll to their large, Victorian-style house located in Key West, Florida.

Robert Eugene Otto's family referred to him as Gene, so he named the doll Robert. Instantly, the two connected. Gene carried the doll everywhere, treating him as one of the family as he played outside and walked the streets. In addition, Gene often spoke to Robert as if he were an actual person and sit him at the dinner table, pretending to feed the doll pieces of his food. For the most part, everything seemed normal as Gene acted towards Robert as most children would to their favorite doll. But as time went on, things took a bizarre turn and Gene's new friend became a terrifying presence.

Gene had entire conversations with Robert. During them, the family heard a strange voice replying to their son. At first, they thought Gene was making the voice himself, but they soon realized the voice they heard was much deeper and sounded different from anything gene could create himself. Not long after, Gene started having terrifying experiences with the doll.

Robert slept in the same bed as Gene. On several occasions, Mr. and Mrs. Otto heard Gene screaming in the middle of the night. As they rushed into the room to see what was happening, they found furniture thrown all over Gene's room. The boy was still in his bed with Robert sat in the corner, seeming to glare at his owner. Once Gene woke, he blamed Robert for the mess. Unfortunately, things would get worse from there.

The family noticed the doll appeared in different locations around the house frequently. And wherever Robert was, they could hear a creepy giggle coming from his direction. As more and more things went missing or were found smashed to pieces, Gene's parents grew increasingly exasperated with him — though he remained insistent that none of it was his fault. He blamed the doll. These events escalated, and soon Gene and his parents weren't the only ones to encounter them. Eventually, stories about the haunted doll spread through the local community, which escalated this home's frightening legacy.

Some neighbors glanced through the house windows and witnessed Robert moving inside the home. Eventually, the Otto family had enough and locked Robert in the attic, sat on a chair looking out an upstairs window. However, this did not stop him from resisting his imprisonment. Guests who visited the home reported hearing footsteps and evil laughter from the attic. Even the neighborhood children passing by the house would avoid staring at the windows, fearing Robert would be staring back at them.

Another unpleasant incident occurred when a plumber visited the home to make repairs. He heard children playing, although nobody but him was inside the house. Investigating the sound, he walked into Gene's room to find Robert sitting there, moving from one side of the bed to the other. After leaving the room, the plumber heard objects being thrown. He rushed back to discover that several toys, that had been on the doll's lap, were now on the other side of the room.

These strange incidents continued through the years. Even in his early adulthood, Gene never let go of Robert. People would see him walking with the doll down the street around age nineteen, talking to it. Something about Robert had a stranglehold on Gene and wasn't about to let him go. One could only wonder, what could have happened to make Robert the doll so malevolent? Or what could have driven Gene to act out, fooling everyone around him into believing his poor behavior was that of an inanimate object? And why, once an adult, was he still trapped in this delusion of his own creation?

Eventually, young Gene grew up, moved out of the home, and went away to art school in Chicago and New York. He became a well-known artist in Key West. Gene made his way to Paris, where he met his wife, Annette Parker. His father eventually passed away, and Gene inherited the family home. He moved back to the US and settled down there once again. Without Robert, Gene had lived a healthy and fulfilling life. Gene had forgotten almost everything about Robert the Doll.

Before he moved into his new home, Gene recovered several childhood items from his parent's home and moved them to his new house with his new family, which included Robert the doll. The past flooded back to him. Like during his childhood, friends and neighbors who visited Gene's home claimed they would sometimes report hearing steps upstairs as if the doll was walking around. Gene found himself once again inseparable from Robert.

Gene quickly got a reputation as an eccentric, wacky artist. His fixation with his childhood doll never truly went away, something his wife despised. Further reports came from children who'd walk past the house on their way to school or home. They reported seeing the doll appear and then vanish from the windows in the dome top of the artist's house, moving around the attic as if it were alive. Many of them feared the house and would steer well clear of it, while other children perceived it as something of an attraction in the neighborhood.

Gene's obsession created great conflict in his marriage. Annette couldn't stand being in the doll's sinister presence. Even with her disapproval of Robert, Gene would place Robert in a chair in the couple's bedroom while they slept, frightening Annette as she woke up to find Robert staring at her. In addition, Annette frequently heard Gene talk to the doll when he was alone with it, sometimes even sounding as if Robert was hurting him and Gene was begging him to stop.

Gene's strange behavior didn't end there. He would often have random, uncontrollable mood swings. He had violent outbursts against his wife and became an abusive man overall. These mood swings ranged from insane rage to completely illogical behavior, then back to his usual self. This odd situation took a toll on Annette, as Gene was physically abusive during these bizarre episodes. At one point, he even locked Annette in the old outhouse for three days. When she got out, he blamed Robert. Gene would proclaim Robert the head of the house, building furniture for him and even demanding that he be fed before anybody else.

Robert Eugene Otto died in 1974, and some stories suggest that even his death was bizarre. In particular, he was found dead in the house's attic, which was by now the quarters designated entirely as Robert's dwelling. Strangly, Robert was supposedly on top of Gene's body with his hands around the man's neck. Soon after that, Annette sold the house and moved back to her homeland, leaving both Roberts behind.

Gene left Robert the doll to Myrtle Reuter, who bought the house and settled in with her young daughter. As Myrtle entered the haunted home, the dreadful process started all over again. Myrtle's ten-year-old daughter soon came across Robert the Doll, who was left collecting dust in his attic, and took a liking to him. Like before, people who went to the house sometimes said strange noises came from the attic, and Myrtle claimed the doll moved around the house.

The woman kept Robert for twenty years before donating it to the Fort East Martello Museum in Florida in 1994, where he remains to this day, kept in a glass box in the building's basement. When Myrtle delivered the doll, she warned the museum that the doll was haunted and should be treated with great care. The museum staff promptly dismissed the advice, but quickly changed their minds when they experienced their own paranormal encounters. The staff reported it seemed as if Robert would wander out of his locked display case, showing up in places he didn't belong.

As he had already become something of an urban legend, Robert attracted scores of people from all over, both skeptics and believers alike. Some say he doesn't like it when people take pictures of him without asking his permission first. It is also said that people who disregard this rule soon suffer from near-fatal car accidents or other kinds of severe misfortunes. These are apology letters from the numerous people who have knowingly crossed his boundaries and suffered the consequences. Some people even leave offerings to Robert, hoping that he will forgive them their transgressions as the years have gone by. Some letters ask Robert for advice. Others were asking for him to place a curse on someone. But, possibly most disturbingly, are the fan letters from children as young as eight years old. Who often include drawn portraits of Robert.

Robert's fame has grown to where he is known by many throughout the internet. He even has a presence on social media, which his caretaker runs on his behalf. Upon visiting Robert, some people claim they feel a dark, dense presence around him. Some even claim to feel a change of expression when looking directly at his face. Robert is now over 110 years old and remains an attraction in the city of Key West.

Some still claim to hear Children's voices at night when the closing staff is still in the museum, along with the sound of running feet and objects being knocked over. Robert continues to be locked in his display case to this day, and is one of the museum's main attractions.

There are several theories about Robert's origin. One was that Gene's grandfather brought Robert home from a trip to Germany and gave to the doll to his grandson as a birthday gift. Which the Steiff company, who produces high-end collector's teddy bears, made Robert the doll in Germany in 1904. However, another theory is a bit darker, which many people believe is the actual origin of the doll.

The Otto family owned a plantation and had many servants who worked on the property. Months before Robert Eugene Otto was born, Mrs. Otto asked Mr. Otto to go to the Bahamas and bring home a few servants to help around the house. She instructed him to ensure that one of them was a woman who could serve as a babysitter for little Gene once he was born. However, Mr. Otto allegedly proved entirely untrustworthy during his trip, and he got the soon-to-be nanny pregnant. Mrs. Otto was believed to be extremely cruel to the woman, punishing her by locking her inside their outhouse for the nine months of her pregnancy, scarcely feeding her.

The woman gave birth to a little girl. However, the baby was very frail due to the mother's malnutrition and other complications, and the child died after two months. Because of this cruel act by Mrs. Otto, the woman carried out a ritual that was an established custom in the Santeria religion. This faith incorporates elements of voodoo and animal sacrifice. They slaughtered a chicken as an offering during this ritual. Using this voodoo magic, some believe she trapped her daughter's spirit inside a doll.

Mrs. Otto caught the servants practicing black magic and quickly fired them in retaliation. The nanny had become attached to young Gene and tried to convince her mistress not to separate them, but was unsuccessful. So, as a farewell gift, the woman gave Gene a doll as revenge for being mistreated by Mrs. Otto.

Whichever of the two stories is true, the gift to Robert Eugene marked the beginning of the horrors and hauntings that were to follow for years. However, many people who are sensitive to spirits have claimed to feel the spirit of a small girl living inside the doll. There have also been sightings of a small girl walking around or sitting on the stairs leading up to the attic where Robert once lived. She is described as being around five years old, dressed in a small white gown, and wearing pigtails. Other people who visit the house have run away in fear after hearing the girl's disembodied laughter from the halls while spending the night.

Whether or not a spirit possesses Robert is up for debate. Those who have seen Robert up the close claim he can move within the glass box, and some even claim he can move out of the glass entirely during the night. Could it be that Gene suffered from severe mental problems from a young age? Some episodes resemble symptoms of a multiple personality disorder. While Robert's true nature can be debated, there's no denying the impact he's made on the paranormal community.

If you're curious to meet Robert in person, you can visit the Fort East Martello Museum in Key West. But you better take our advice and mind your manners when you do.

CHAPTER 8:
LOST AT SEA–THE REAL PIRATES OF THE CARIBBEAN

W E HAVE TALKED ABOUT STORIES OF BOTH INDIVIDUAL AND GROUP HAUNTINGS. Our next intriguing adventure involves the entire crew of a ghost ship! Chances are, you have heard about the *Flying Dutchman* from the Disney blockbuster series, *Pirates of the Caribbean*. The storyline in the movie draws from myths of seafaring pirates, wherein the legendary Davy Jones has been tasked to captain the equally legendary ghost ship, the *Flying Dutchman*. While the history of the pirate idiom "Davy Jones' locker" refers to sailors plunging to their deaths at the bottom of the sea, the *Flying Dutchman* actually existed.

In the 17th century, a company called the Dutch East India Company was responsible for considerable trade over the oceans. It's believed that the vessel in question, the *Flying Dutchman*, initially sailed for this company. George Barrington penned the first written record found to mention the ship, entitled *An Account of a Voyage to New South Wales*. Following is his account of the story:

"The superstition of the sailors was a subject of which I had frequently heard, and even the report that agitated the person of whom I am going to speak, but I thought it too vague to deserve any particular credit or attention. In this quarter of the globe, it seems, a report is still propagated, that some years ago a Dutchman of war lost off the Cape, every soul on board perished. Being in company with another vessel, this, her consort weathered the gale, and more fortunate, arrived soon after at the Cape. But having repaired their damages and returning to Europe, just in the same latitude, they were likewise overtaken with a heavy gale. They reported a vessel crowding down upon them during the night watch with a full press of sail as if she intended nothing but to run them down. One of the people in particular, positively affirmed, that it was the ship foundered in the recent gale of her apparition. The weather very soon after clearing up, the real object, a thick dark cloud, entirely disappeared. Still, nothing could dispose of the minds of the sailors of what they fancied they had seen; and they had no sooner got into port, then spreading the story like wildfire, the supposed phantom obtained the name of the *Flying Dutchman*. From the Dutch, the English seamen got hold of the story; so that very few of our East-Indiamen pass those seas, without having someone on board, who persuades himself that he also has seen the apparition (Barrington, p.116-117)."[1]

Barrington goes on to describe how the lead crewman of his vessel woke him in the middle of the night, telling him of the ghostly apparition he had seen just minutes before, in full belief that what he saw was indeed the *Flying Dutchman.*

It is thought that the captains of the two ships described by Barrington were Hendrik Van der Decken and Bernard Fokke, both of whom were captains for the Dutch East India Company. However, it is still unclear who in the story is the captain of the surviving ship, and who became captain of the *Flying Dutchman,* as both were said to have been lost at sea. We are aware of Van der Decken, and we know Fokke made many voyages from the Netherlands to Java and at incredible speeds.

Some surmise that Fokke made a pact with the devil, wherein he received the momentum he needed for his trading activities. If this were indeed true, it would be plausible that the captain would wager his own life and that of his crew and sail on even when faced with a storm as he approached the Cape of Good Hope. Hence the belief that Captain Bernard Fokke was none other than the fearless captain of the *Flying Dutchman.*

There have been many tales spun around this ship and its journey. When the vessel came upon a gale at sea, some have rumored that Fokke threw men overboard to appease the storm. Some say that the captain vowed he would sail the seas forever until he rounded the Cape of Good Hope, but was tragically shipwrecked, thus drowning all hope of making it to safety. Because of his stubbornness, the story goes that he and his crew were cursed to endlessly sail the oceans, never once being allowed to rest, nor to set foot on any shore.

You might think that an entire ghost ship is impossible. I say to you, tell that to the hundreds of witnesses who had sightings of the famous Dutch vessel over the many years. Notable people who saw the *Flying Dutchman* firsthand include King George V of England and the renowned novelist Nicholas Monsarrat. The legend is that those unfortunate to see it are doomed to befall calamity, or worse, death. So, should you find yourself out to sea chasing some adventure, beware you never come within viewing distance to the *Flying Dutchman*.

CHAPTER 9:
DARKNESS BENEATH THE CITY OF LIGHT

WHEN WE THINK OF PARIS NOWADAYS, many of us turn to thoughts of love, culture, and French cuisine. We may also think of landmarks such as the Eiffel Tower, the Louvre, and other cultural marvels of this famed city. Indeed, this renowned metropolis has a lot to offer to visitors. However, as you may or may not know, there is a great deal that lies beneath the city streets as well.

Aside from its subway network and old mining tunnels, the underground of Paris has a frighteningly intricate web of ancient catacombs. The nature of these catacombs is such that they are an ominous place regardless of whether they have actual ghosts or demons stalking their long corridors. While ghostly haunting is not out of the question, there is one thing you can count on—

these catacombs have a dark and disturbing history. The tunnels cumulatively are a few hundred miles long and are the eternal home to the remains of around six million people.

The catacombs, established in the first half of the 18th century, are a disturbing sight to see. The thing about these halls of the dead is that for a lot — if not most — of the souls that inhabit them, the catacombs weren't their rightly intended resting place. These catacombs were built to transfer the unburied remains from the city cemeteries for several reasons.

The cemeteries were crowded beyond capacity and numerous gravesites in the city collapsed, making disease and other contamination a genuine threat. The overflow of bodies from these issues caused authorities to move many of the dead into the underground in the period between the late eighteenth and mid nineteenth centuries, disturbing their peace in the process. Most of the remains would be mere bones by the time they were approved for transportation, and all this was conducted under the veil of darkness.

Some skulls and bones are stacked perfectly along the walls of the tunnels, giving an artistic quality to them. Other remains were thrown, dumped, or scattered in small rooms and tunnels, leaving them piled up in no order. It's safe to say one can find human bones almost anywhere in the catacombs.

If there is a place in the world where ghosts and wandering souls are likely to lurk, it's here. The countless number of human remains relocated to the catacombs are fuel for stories and theories. Over the years, visitors made widespread reports of what they believed were sightings and encounters with ghosts.

Some have described an unrelenting feeling of being watched and stalked while underground, while others even said they felt somebody or something physically touching them. But if there is something paranormal to be seen down there, one must take quite a few risks to get to the position of catching anything.

The Catacombs of Paris have been open to the public since the nineteenth century and are accessible via a designated exterior entrance. This section of the catacombs is the staging area for organized tours. However, these tours are limited both in their longevity and their area, as they only focus on a tiny portion of the vast system. This tour provides tourists and other curious cats with a basic idea of the sights, ambiance, and the isolation of the catacombs, but it all amounts to just a taste of the real thing in the end.

People who have ventured into restricted areas of the catacombs do so at the risk of their own life and are breaking the law. The Paris catacombs can be accessed from several locations apart from the formal entrance. In addition, there are utility holes and similar openings all over the city that lead into the catacombs. Using these access points and venturing beyond the designated touring areas is illegal and carries with it a fine, which is much less than what a lot of enthusiasts will risk for their thrills.

Apart from a slight run-in with the law, exploring the catacombs poses many real dangers and can cost those who dare embark upon such a journey way more than a small amount of money. Since a considerable portion of the catacombs is off limits, it is not illuminated, refurbished, or secured. The tunnels can get very confusing, even if you have a map, and the absolute, enveloping darkness one would face only makes this worse. Another threat is that some parts of the catacombs may be unstable and prone to collapse or flooding. Short of getting killed outright, one can quickly lose your way and get lost, which may result in a slow, excruciating death over days or weeks.

One man ventured into the remote parts of the catacombs alone. He started on his journey in the early 1990s. Footage was retrieved from the man's camera, which was the only trace of him ever found. He brought this camera with him to document his journey using the camera's night vision.

The man seemed well-adjusted, determined, organized, and entirely in control for most of the forty minute recording he left behind. He documented many corridors and bones in the crypts as he proceeded deeper into the underbelly of Paris. The footage revealed markings on the walls, mostly arrows, which the explorer seemed to follow. It wasn't until a while into the footage that things took a strange turn and quickly spiraled out of hand. The daring individual moved through the tunnels more erratically, soon falling into a state of outright panic. At first, it appeared as though he had lost his way and became terrified. However, his behavior soon resembled that of a person panicking and running from something. He turned around to look back a few times, while the camera caught glimpses of more markings or drawings on the walls. The most interesting of which depicted a person with outstretched limbs, painted on in white.

After a while of frantically rushing about through the crypts, the man did something incredibly strange. He simply dropped his camera, and it seemed to fall into a small puddle of water, while still recording, showing the man running into the darkness ahead of it. This peculiar action further argues the case that he was not merely lost. Discarding his only source of light while lost in utter darkness seems illogical and outright insane. In the likelihood that he dropped the camera by accident, the question begged is, why didn't he think to pick it up? Thus, it is possible that he was running from something or someone. But if so, from whom? Or what?

This story broke into the mainstream media and was featured on television. There has been significant debate over whether the footage is genuine. Furthermore, a group of explorers later entered the tunnels hoping to find and record the same locations seen in the footage. They succeeded and recorded the same markings and images on the walls, including the strange white figure. But controversy has lingered over the question of how real the original man's footage is. Some speculate it was a staged prank. A man may have simply gone in, recorded footage of himself acting as though he is panicking, and dropped the camera for others to find and ponder over.

Whatever the case may be, nobody has ever come forward to claim authorship of the footage, and there have been cases of people getting lost in the catacombs during their history, never to be found again. This incident may undoubtedly be yet another such tragedy. If the footage wasn't staged, it's possible that there was more to this man's tragic fate than just losing his way in the dark.

It might take many years for us to find out what happened to him. Until that happens, we may assume his fate adds one more set of remains to the six million already lost within the catacombs. On the other hand, the man may have gotten out fine that very day, having quite a laugh expecting someone to find the footage and make it public. The recording has since been uploaded to the internet for all to see and judge on their own, and something tells me it will not strike you as a joke.

CHAPTER 10:
HAUNTED EBAY PAINTING

HAUNTINGS CAN OCCUR ANYWHERE, BUT ARE MOST OFTEN ASSOCIATED with a particular place where paranormal activity is widespread. This haunting, however, is that of a painting. Apparently, even the artwork hanging in your home can become haunted. This haunting is also one of the most recent and well-known modern hauntings, and the story will leave chills running down your spine.

William Stoneham, the painter of this haunted canvas, is still alive, well, and painting today. He was born in Boston, Massachusetts, where his birth parents gave him up for adoption. The painting is that of a photograph taken of him when he was only five years old. The creepy artwork, titled *The Hands Resist Him*, depicts a young boy and a young female doll holding a battery-like object with wires, standing together in front of a glass door with images of hands seemingly floating behind the glass panels. The painter himself agrees that it may be a haunted painting. He claims on his website that he always had a particular connection to the collective unconscious found in a specific place. According to Stoneham, "The hands are the 'other lives'. The glass door, that thin veil between waking and dreaming. The doll is the imagined companion or guides through this realm."[2] According to Stoneham, the inspiration for the painting came from the following poem titled "Hands Resist Him", penned in 1971 by R. Ponseti, Bill's ex-wife, just three years before the creation of the painting:

He is of seeing visions.

His strokes reveal them.

In a rush- of color, of madness

Of mystics

And his head is the highest center.

It must confront its enemy,

The hands- resist him,

like the secret of his birth.

His presence is the sanctum heartbeat.

Felt in darkness and passion.

It's sound the sole gift to that silence.[3]

Whether you believe in ghosts or not, looking at the painting may give you the creeps. In the image, the boy's eyes are almost non-existent, as if he is squinting. His pale skin appears sickly or even lifeless. The doll has hollowed-out eyes. She is frowning, and some say her countenance resembles that of an evil spirit. These details alone are eerie enough, but it doesn't stop there. Behind the two figures, inside a dark room, are dozens of little hands grasping at the glass panes of the door. No bodies are visible, and it appears as if the hands are floating. Or perhaps, those locked within the darkness are pressing against the glass, seeking escape from the abyss within. They seem disembodied, trying to claw their way outside. Altogether, many find the painting to be unsettling.

Little did Stoneham know that what he created would become something of a legend. After he completed the painting, it was sold to John Marley—an actor credited with over a hundred film and television appearances, including several episodes of The Twilight Zone. He is probably best known for his role as a producer for the legendary film *The Godfather*.

When he purchased the painting, becoming the subject of a real-life Twilight Zone episode was probably the furthest thing from his mind. Within the next ten years, three people who dealt with the painting suddenly died: Henry J. Seldis, an immigrant from Germany and the art critic who gave the piece its first press mention. Charles M. Feingarten, the owner of the gallery where the painting was initially displayed and who originally commissioned the piece. And finally, Marley himself, but not until after he sold the painting.

The Hands Resist Him vanished from the headlines for the next twenty six years. It then resurfaced in an eBay listing. According to an article published by the BBC[4], the owners were selling the painting due to its haunted nature. They stated the children in the picture came alive at night, stepping out into the real world.

They found the painting in the possession of a collector who found it behind an abandoned bar. They reinforced their eBay listing with footage and photos from a webcam capturing these strange happenings at night. The Internet was abuzz with rumors in just a few days, and the listing had garnered over thirty thousand page views. Reports from all over came out, claiming people that viewed the video experienced strange occurrences such as illness and fainting. Kim Smith, the owner of an art gallery in Grand Rapids, Michigan, finally purchased the painting.

Since his purchase, Kim has reported no kind of paranormal activity associated with the picture. However, it is notable that it remains in storage and has only been shown, on request, to a handful of people.

But what if the spirits in the painting are merely lying dormant, waiting for the opportunity to strike again? After all, it laid dormant for twenty six years before wreaking terror on the lives of the family that just so happened to purchase it. Will the year 2026 bring new and frightening news about the painting? This much is true: Whether you believe that the art is possessed or not, many who have viewed *The Hands Resist Him* agree that that is a creepy, haunting image.

CHAPTER 11:
THE REAL ANNABELLE

THE WARRENS' OCCULT MUSEUM BELONGS TO A PAIR of the most famous paranormal investigators in the world. Over the years, they have undertaken numerous paranormal cases, taken the most haunted and dangerous objects they've uncovered, and placed them in this occult museum in Connecticut. In a large glass cabinet sits an old, worn-out Raggedy Ann rag doll. However, this is no ordinary doll. It's surrounded by warnings asking people to stay away, and anyone who's been in its presence will tell you it's the scariest item of them all. Its name is Annabelle. The toy doll may come across as reasonably creepy, especially when you know the story behind it.

You've may have heard the name Annabelle from a popular series of movies called The Conjuring, based on the adventures of real-life paranormal investigators Ed and Lorraine Warren. The Warrens have since passed on, but their legacy is only growing thanks to their museum and the movies. However, the real story of Annabelle and how she wound up at the Warrens' museum tells a quite different story.

The story begins in 1970 with a young woman named Donna. She lived in a small apartment with her roommate, Angie. On Donna's twenty-eighth birthday, she received a gift from her mother. It was a Raggedy Ann Doll. Donna loved the doll, brought it home to her apartment, and placed it on the couch in their living room. As days went on, the women noticed the doll in different spots than where they originally put her. They would place her in the corner of the couch before leaving for work. When they came back, they would find the doll in an impossible location, for instance, in another locked room. However, that wasn't the only thing odd that was happening. They soon started finding notes around the home saying, "Help Me!" What made the notes even stranger was that they were all written on parchment paper, which the women didn't have in their apartment. As strange as it may sound, Donna grew accustomed to the doll's antics and didn't take them seriously. However, that was about to change.

Angie's fiancé Lou would often visit her at the apartment. So often, she gave him a key. At first sight of the doll, he suggested Donna throw it out because he felt something evil. Donna wasn't about to throw away a gift from her mother, so they ignored Lou's warnings. But one day Lou started having recurring nightmares about Annabelle. In his dream, He opened his eyes was completely paralyzed. All he could do was look around the room. He looked down at his feet and saw Annabelle standing there. She slowly crawled up his legs and to his chest, where she strangled him. Unable to move, Lou panicked as he struggled to breathe. Then everything got dark, and he passed out. When he woke, Lou felt it wasn't a dream. It felt too real.

After Lou told Donna and Angie about the dream, they agreed they needed help. So, they scheduled a session with a local psychic medium hoping to obtain answers. The medium attempted to establish communication with any spirits that may have attached themselves to the doll. She claimed to have discovered a ghost of a little girl named Annabelle Higgins possessed the doll. This girl was seven years old and was found dead in the same area Donna's home stood. She also explained that the little girls' spirit wanted to be nurtured by Donna and her roommate. The story touched Donna, so she decided she could live with this and keep Annabelle.

A few weeks after Lou's dream, he and Angie were alone in their apartment planning a road trip. Suddenly, they heard an unusual sound coming from Donna's bedroom. It instantly caught Angie's attention because Donna wasn't home. So, Lou investigated. He pressed his ear to the door to make out what the noise was. Soon after doing that, it stopped. Lou pushed open the door and inspected the room for any signs of a break-in. He noticed Annabelle sitting on the floor, but besides that, nothing seemed misplaced or tampered with. However, Lou claimed a strange feeling came over him as soon as he stepped closer to Annabelle. Lou had the feeling that someone was standing behind him. As Lou turned to walk out, he suddenly felt a sharp pain in his chest. When he looked under his shirt, he found bloody claw marks across his upper body. He didn't know how he got the slashes on his chest; there was no one in the room. Oddly enough, after two days, Lou said the claw marks mysteriously vanished. Besides Lou's experience, Angie noticed bloodstains unexplainably appearing on the doll's hands or dress.

This incident led the trio to seek help once again. Donna suspected something other than the spirit of a little girl who just wanted to be cared for possessed Annabelle, based on how malicious she became. Donna got a hold of a priest, who then forwarded her to his superior, Father Cooke. Based on Donna and Angie's description of their encounters, Cooke knew this was something very evil and he needed help. He got in touch with paranormal investigators Ed and Lorraine Warren.

The Warrens scheduled a time to meet with Donna and her roommate to discuss the details of the incidents. They soon arrived at the apartment with Father Cooke. Donna, Angie, and Lou described the strange things happening around the apartment after they received Annabelle. The Warrens told Donna that struggling human spirits rarely possess objects or people. Instead, they usually wander and haunt locations. They further explained that what possesses objects or people is a demonic presence. These demonic forces hold an object and use them as a temporary intermediary while seeking a human soul. In this case, the soul that this demon desired was Donna's.

Cooke and the Warrens agreed to perform an exorcism ritual to banish the demonic spirit from the apartment, and hopefully the doll itself. They conducted the exorcism according to traditional rites and recitations. Still, the Warrens asked Donna to let go of the toy doll and let them take it just in case the exorcism didn't work. Donna agreed, and the Warrens took possession of the troublesome toy. It seemed, however, that whatever was taking hold of the doll was far from gone. As soon as the Warrens put Annabelle in the vehicle, strange things happened. As they drove away, they headed along narrow windy roads down a mountain when the power steering and brakes unexpectedly stopped working. The vehicle was new, and it didn't show any signs of a problem before encountering the doll. The only way they could get home was by showering holy water around the doll.

They brought it with them and, according to the Warrens, took precautions for their safety, such as avoiding the highway on their way home. But their suspicions proved right, and the doll continued to be possessed by the dark force. In addition, the couple reported having minor, strange problems with their car not long after they departed.

The Warren's took the doll home, where they intended to keep it. However, they reported Annabelle brought strange incidents to their home in much of the same ways she did while Donna had her. So, they brought in another priest and asked him to attempt an exorcism on Annabelle.

At the second exorcism, the priest didn't take Annabelle seriously, despite Ed's warnings. Instead, the priest mocked her, saying she was a hoax. Before leaving the Warrens' home, Lorraine warned the priest to drive carefully. Unfortunately, on his way home, the priest's brakes mysteriously failed, and he lost control of his vehicle, driving straight into oncoming traffic. This destroyed his vehicle and sent him to the hospital in critical condition.

The exorcism didn't seem to have had any long-lasting effects on Annabelle. The Warrens had to confine the haunted doll once and for all. They built a special glass case with a roof and a cross on top, resembling a church.

The Warrens were always incredibly careful about keeping people away from the case. Ed placed a warning sign on the case that reads, "Warning, positively do not open." Most visitors respect the warning. However, there was a man who didn't and paid the price for it. A skeptical young man visited the museum one day. Despite the warnings, he didn't seem to be afraid of Annabelle at all.

The man got close to Annabelle's case, laugh at her, demanded the doll to cut him, and even knock on her case, but nothing happened. The staff immediately asked him to leave, so the young man left with his girlfriend on their motorcycle. The girlfriend later stated that they were laughing about the doll when the motorcycle spiraled out of control, and they crashed into a tree. The girlfriend survived the crash, but the young man died instantly. The Warrens believe this was Annabelle's first murder.

Annabelle is currently locked away in the Warrens' Occult Museum in Monroe, Connecticut, along with many other trophies and artifacts they collected in their line of work dealing with the paranormal. The museum is currently closed since the death of Lorraine Warren. Tony Spera, Warren's son-in-law, oversees the museum and has yet to reopen it.

Of course, you should always take stories with a healthy dose of skepticism, and everybody is right to do so. However, it is best not to push your luck and challenge the unseen forces that may well exist, forces that we do not understand.

CHAPTER 12:
DORIS BITHER

IF YOU'RE A FAN OF HORROR FLICKS, THE CHANCES ARE THAT you have heard of 1982's *The Entity*. Many are unaware the writers of this horror film based it on real events. In the chilling story, a paranormal force that turns out to be a demon sexually assaults a woman. The movie is based on a book of the same name, written in the late 1970s. This, in turn, took after the alleged haunting that befell Doris Bither, starting early in the same decade, in Culver City, California.

As investigators who handled Doris' case from 1974 later revealed, the woman lived a life of hardship and abuse long before supernatural torment was upon her too. Doris was forced out of her home at a young age and had to make her way the best she could. She had also involved in many dysfunctional relationships, with a lot of them turning abusive. Doris also brought additional trouble on herself in adolescence. She gained an interest in ghosts and often attempted to spawn them via Ouija boards and other methods.

After years of trials and tribulations, Doris eventually fell into substance abuse, especially alcohol, which persisted for most of her life. This and her deep emotional scars contributed to the arguments made by many skeptics later, who believed Doris wasn't of sound mind. However, Doris was far from alone in witnessing the hauntings, especially after investigators became involved.

At first, the case appeared to be a regular instance of haunting and piqued the interest of renowned parapsychologist and paranormal investigator Dr. Barry Taff. In the summer of 1974, Taff and his associate Kerry Gaynor were engaged in conversation on paranormal phenomena at a bookstore. It was then that Doris Bither walked up to them and said she believed her house was haunted, and that she'd like them to investigate it. The details she provided intrigued the investigators, but she didn't tell them the whole story at that time. The interest was enough to motivate a visit, though, and they went to her house on August 22.

When they arrived, they noted the poor living conditions in the neglected home. Doris, a single mother, had four children from four different fathers living in the house. Doris' daughter was only six, and her three sons were ten, thirteen, and sixteen. It was also apparent to Taff and Gaynor that the mother had a strained relationship with her male children, especially the teens.

The investigators started by interviewing Doris, which went on for a couple of hours as she described the anomalies her family experienced in the house. There was allegedly activity associated with poltergeists, but some particularly disturbing details included her and the children bumping into ghosts. As Dr. Taff later explained in an interview he gave on television, he couldn't shake the feeling that Doris omitted an essential aspect of the story while they talked.

Ultimately, Doris opened up and the story turned to a new shade of disturbing and vile. She explained there were three ghosts of Asian men who hunted and assaulted her. The trio consisted of two smaller specters who would restrain her with overwhelming force, while the third, larger poltergeist assaulted her. She also mentioned one instance where her oldest son tried to defend her but was subdued and thrown away by the invisible assailants, injuring his arm. As for the very existence of these entities, it supported testimonies from neighbors, who claimed to have indeed seen apparitions around Doris' home.

Regarding the alleged rape, Doris presented evidence to the investigators. She showed them severe bruising on her inner thighs and several other places on her body. It appeared the ghosts were almost a regular occurrence around the home, as the children were all aware of their existence. One spirit even earned a nickname of "Mr. Whose-It" from the kids.

Barry Taff was interested, but was highly skeptical of certain aspects of her story, especially the allegations of spectral rape. This notion was the first time he and Gaynor heard such a thing from a victim of a haunting. Regardless, Taff and Gaynor summoned their team to the house and set up their equipment hoping to detect and possibly capture some evidence.

After Taff made the calls, there were around thirty investigators on location, including photographers. They then told Doris to summon her spectral tormentors, which she did by calling out and cursing them. Reportedly, orbs and arcs of light materialized in the room. The team took photographs and recorded the phenomena, but capturing anything clear proved difficult because the lights were difficult to frame. As Taff explained in a later interview, each time they snapped a photo, the developed photographs turned out almost entirely white, obviously blinded by some sort of flash.

He showed these photographs in the same interview, including a couple of pictures that caught an arc of light across the photo. In one image he presented, on a corner, the background has an arc spanning the image without bending, proving that it wasn't light from a flashlight projecting onto the wall. The bright white arc in this black-and-white picture encircled Doris from overhead as she sat on the bed in the corner.

This interference with the cameras also occurred when they tried to photograph what Doris was insisting was a ghost. She kept pointing at something she said she was seeing, but nobody else noticed anything. Doris would frantically yell that "it" was right in front of her face. Barry explained they tried to capture whatever it might have been with their Polaroid instant cameras, again getting flashed-out pictures. Curiously enough, Barry got the idea to take photos when Doris was not near and compare the results. Sure enough, the images taken when Doris wasn't around were perfectly normal. All the while, pungent, disgusting smells emitted randomly from different sources, usually coming from where Doris would point.

Amid these confrontations, the team also described a mysterious green mist that emerged in one corner, spreading upwards and ultimately forming what looked like a silhouette of a muscular male torso. Upon seeing this, one member of the team reportedly fainted.

They spent a couple of months observing and documenting what Barry Taff described as a "plethora of phenomena during the investigation." The anomalies decreased in intensity and frequency as time went by.

There were a few critical facts about Doris that related to the case and could explain the phenomenon. Barry Taff put a lot of effort into explaining what was happening, and he developed some interesting theories in that regard.

First, as we've mentioned, Doris had a drinking problem which she refused to address all her life. Doris's drinking was her way of living with the figurative demons within, birthed from so much trauma that she endured in life. Her childhood was a reel of abuse and hardship which left profound scars on her mind. Things got worse as she entered adulthood and became involved in relationships. After all, she had four children, none of whose fathers were around to help. Because of her emotional problems and possible mistrust towards men, her relationship with her sons was dysfunctional.

Taff stated that all of this played a crucial part in the hauntings. Foremost, Taff remained skeptical of the concept of "spectral rape" to the very end. He didn't dismiss that the poltergeists had attacked Doris, but he offered his theory about what exactly was at work. He noted that the paranormal activity would start and be most intense around Doris when she was under the influence. In contrast, things would usually be normal when she was sober.

Barry Taff further explained that he believed these poltergeists were psychosomatic — manifestations of Doris' inner turmoil and emotional baggage, such as rage, pain, depression, and addiction. More importantly, he expressed his belief that Doris had psychokinetic powers. When combined with her inner demons and negative energy, especially when unhinged during an alcoholic stupor, this in those demons manifesting themselves the physical world. This idea meant they affected her directly, which Barry explains, resulted in Doris believing she was raped. He saw this assault as a projection of Doris' suppressed trauma and experiences of abuse, as well as the toxic energy between her and the three boys she was raising, which resembles Doris' account of precisely three spectral assailants.

Some believe that psychokinetic powers are hereditary. Therefore, the theory that Doris's sons and their negative feelings towards Doris, her neglect, and her addiction, channeled even more power into the pool of paranormal energy and abnormal activity in the household. If the family indeed possessed psychokinetic powers, it's also possible that the three ghosts were figments of the minds of her sons themselves, as they inadvertently projected their anger onto the mother with terrifying results. These paranormal attacks could have triggered memories and were then perceived by drunken Doris as rape, since there is a good possibility that she had lived through sexual assault during her life.

Essentially, what all of this means is that Dr. Taff believed Doris herself could have been the source of the phenomena surrounding her. The psychokinetic power of her mind channeled the contents of her subconscious mind right into the real world, without her even knowing it or being able to control it. Of course, Barry Taff didn't claim this as the ultimate truth, nor did he state he had apparent answers. Still, he feels that this interesting possibility appealed the most to the fascinating case of Doris Bither.

One last detail supports his theory. Namely, the phenomena reportedly ceased in the house after Doris left, and no subsequent residents reported anything strange. Doris moved twice throughout California, went to Texas at one point, and eventually settled in San Bernardino. However, she reported that her ghostly persecutors followed her everywhere she went. If this was indeed the case, then Taff may have been correct.

Whatever the explanation was, the life of Doris Bither was a jagged string of hardship and misfortune. Her apparent confrontation with the forces beyond only added to the suffering. Regardless, that she sought help from Barry Taff and Kerry Gaynor showed that she had a will to fight her demons, and it also gave Taff one of the fascinating cases among thousands he has investigated to date. The case stays with him to this day and continues to haunt all those involved. As for Doris, one of her sons has reported that she died back in 1999, at the age of only fifty-nine, from respiratory complications. Whatever waits for us beyond our realm after we pass, we can only hope that Doris has finally found peace from both the symbolic and actual ghosts that had haunted her for all her life. If the unfortunate can't find solace and refuge in this life, it's comforting to believe that it at least comes after we are put to rest.

CHAPTER 13:
AMITYVILLE HORROR HOUSE

THE STORY OF THE HAUNTED HOUSE IN AMITYVILLE, New York is one of the most publicized cases involving the Warren couple and their paranormal investigations. It has spawned and inspired a few famous movies, such as the 1979's *The Amityville Horror* and the 2005 remake. This fame and the overreaching nature of Hollywood may be why it is challenging to know what happened in the Amityville house. Perhaps, that it is arguably a fascinating story causes both controversy and popularity. Then again, just about every ghost sighting or haunting is with skepticism. Either way, it is quite a terrifying tale of a haunted house—a place already cursed with so much evil documented to have happened on the premises.

This dark history has undoubtedly left its mark on the suburban home in Amityville The only question is whether this maliciousness exists through something more than just a memory of human darkness. In November 1974, Ronald DeFeo Jr. murdered his parents, two brothers, and two sisters in cold blood. He executed the victims in their beds during the night, with a rifle. DeFeo tried to mask his atrocity by going to the local bar and "looking for help", proclaiming that someone murdered his parents. Unfortunately, the ammunition used in the killings was in DeFeo's possession, and police arrested him. He further claimed that he didn't know his siblings were murdered as well when he went to the bar to seek help.

All these accounts of DeFeo were, as far as everybody was concerned, complete lies. He was found guilty of six counts of second-degree murder and given six consecutive terms of twenty-five years to life for his harrowing crimes, which he still serves.

However, DeFeo gave varying testimonies regarding what happened at the house. His defense attorney attempted an insanity plea, claiming that DeFeo heard voices in his head that told him to commit the crime. Overall, he was inconsistent, blaming his sister and even an outside perpetrator at times. The DA disregarding all these allegations as fabrications, and his sentences stood. It's safe to assume he murdered his family. But some of the particulars of the case are strange.

Namely, all six victims were found in bed, face down. One would expect the rest of the family would take notice as soon as Ronald fired the first shot, but the positions that the bodies were in suggest that they didn't react at all. The police investigators were troubled by the same speculations in the beginning. How could one man move fast enough to execute six people in their beds before the noise woke any of them? One possible explanation was that the family was sedated, but toxicology results refuted this theory. Furthermore, it's particularly strange that no neighbor reported hearing gunfire, and the police confirmed there was no suppressor on the weapon used.

Whatever the details of that night may be, it's believed that horrifying event caused the alleged haunting of the house by evil spirits.

The Lutz family moved into the house a little over a year after the murders. They were aware of the horrendous past that plagued the home, but they were fond of the house's Dutch colonial style and the price was appealing to them. The Lutz family included George and Kathy, and three children from Kathy's previous marriage: Daniel, Missy, and Christopher.

On the day they moved in, Kathy requested that a Catholic priest bless their new home. It was then that the first paranormal reports began. While the priest was sprinkling holy water throughout the house, he went into the room previously used by two of the DeFeo boys, Marc and John. Allegedly, the priest heard a deep, unsettling voice talking to him, warning him to leave the house. He complied, but he didn't tell the family what he experienced. Instead, he simply left them with an ominous warning not to use that room for sleeping under any circumstance. They took his advice and designated it a sewing room.

In 1979, a television show called *In Search Of* supposedly tracked down the priest in question and invited him to give an interview on the program. The priest agreed, but he demanded that he remain anonymous, so his face was hidden.

He described the experience, explaining the room felt strange the moment he walked in. He said it was much colder than one would expect, and that the voice talked to him as he started sprinkling his holy water. The priest quoted the demonic voice as merely saying, "Get out!" Furthermore, he described a physical sensation right after that. This sensation was like a slap on his face, even though he was alone in the room. In the interview, he also claimed cysts or blisters appeared on his hands shortly after that incident.

The episode also shared how the priest tried to call the family later on, to warn them of the full scope of the evil threat in their house. However, there seemed to always be something wrong with the phone connection, and unyielding static prevented any clear communication.

After the priest left and the family finished settling in, trouble began that very night. From that moment, many aspects of their life deteriorated. At first, they experienced all kinds of strange feelings, both physical and mental. Then, they became more irritable and uneasy, leading to tension and arguments in the home. George talked about how he could never seem to warm up, feeling a persistent cold in his bones when he was at home, regardless of how much he tried to keep the fire on and raise the temperature in the house. Daniel and most others involved mentioned these random, cold areas within the house. The couple also said that even their physical health worsened over time.

Their young daughter, Missy, behaved in a oddly as well. She became a shut-in and spent a lot of time in her room all alone, at least as far as anybody else thought. However, Missy claimed she was not alone, but had a friend named Jodie who stayed her most of the time. Of course, everyone else perceived Jodie as an imaginary friend, which is a relatively typical occurrence with young children. Missy described Jodie in different ways, most notably as a pig with glowing red eyes and an angel-type being. Supposedly, Jodie could change her form and size. Missy described her as sometimes being enormous, more prominent than even their house. She also explained that Jodie only made herself visible to whom she wanted, while being completely invisible otherwise.

Although other family members see Jodie in some parts of the *Amityville* movies, nobody reported seeing her in real life. The film also depicts an onslaught of massive swarms of flies in the house. In 2005, *Inside Edition* interviewed the family and asked whether the flies appeared. Christopher and Daniel both said that there were, an unusual number of flies at their home, particularly in the sewing room, but that the movies greatly exaggerated the amount.

The family also described strange, unpleasant smells that spread randomly, their source a mystery. George Lutz also talked about black spots appearing on the ceramics in their bathroom and their toilet bowl. There were also reports of peculiar substances of unknown origin appearing in different locations in the home, but there was never any blood trickling down the walls like in the movie—also confirmed by George. Much like the priest's experience, where he felt some mysterious force slapped him, Kathy also mentioned apparent physical contact. Someone or something that she could not see allegedly touched her.

The Lutz family confirmed as real a few other things in the *Amityville* movie. Namely, Daniel said a window smashed into his hand at one point, and one of his fingers is still deformed because of the injury. Christopher explained later that the windows in the house would often open and shut on their own, although none of them ever broke. The infamous red room exists as well, although it may have been over-dramatized on screen. The red room is a small storage compartment under the stairs leading into the basement.

George woke up to a hair-raising sight on one night. His wife appeared to have changed into a frightening old hag, which horrified him. George would often wake up in the middle of the night and had many sleepless nights. He claimed he would routinely wake up at precisely 3:15 in the morning, which was believed to be around when DeFeo committed the murders. On another occasion, George said he saw his wife levitating above their bed, after which he heard loud noises coming from his children's rooms as if their beds were being moved around with force. When he wanted to investigate what was going on, he found himself paralyzed in bed, unable to lift a single finger.

The family also attempted to get in touch with the priest who blessed the house and ask for help. However, the phone would always seem to experience technical problems when they tried to talk to him. Allegedly, when they tried to banish the spirits with their crucifix, they were told by otherworldly voices to stop what they were doing immediately.

The night that pushed the family over the edge was particularly shocking. There were incredibly loud noises everywhere in the house and furniture moved and was tossed around, terrifying the couple and the children. Finally, they decided they couldn't take it anymore.

It took only twenty-eight days for the Lutz family to vacate the premises, and they temporarily stayed with Kathy's mother. George later told of the horrors they experienced, and he said that it might have been this evil presence that pushed Ronald DeFeo to murder his family. This possibility made him more sympathetic towards the murderer, and he believed his insanity plea might have been real. Despite this, DeFeo later admitted that all his talk of voices commanding him to kill were fabrications and part of his attempt to be acquitted because of insanity.

Twenty days after the Lutz family left the house, a reporter working on the story called in the Warren couple to help with the investigation. They brought in a team, but the Lutz family, the Warrens claimed, would not enter the house during the investigation.

Ed Warren said that an unseen force knocked him down on the floor in the basement, and his wife talked about feeling an incredibly evil presence in the house—a demonic presence. During their investigations, the Warrens discovered that the home built in 1924 and belonged to a John Ketchum, who was involved in black magic and requested to be buried on the grounds.

A different investigation involved a medium visiting the house, who claimed that he established contact with the spirit of a Native American chieftain who was tormenting all who resided on the premises. His reason for this, the medium explained, was anger over the fact that the house was built on a sacred burial ground. However, the natives of the Montaukett tribe still living on Long Island spoke out against this theory, explaining that they had no written record of these grounds used for burial. The tribe also took offense with what the medium said, calling it a baseless assumption that a spirit of their dead would commit itself to evil, which they said would not happen.

Either way, the Warrens maintained that the Lutz's accounts were real and that the haunting resulted from some dark history on the land. The evidence, both for and against the haunting stories, has been debated ever since. The haunting of Amityville remains one of the most famous American cases of its nature, and the Lutz family were the last occupants to experience these terrors and speak out about them.

One of the central questions of the matter thus presents itself: If the story was a hoax, what finally drove the Lutz family to hurriedly vacate the premises less than a month after moving in? As is generally the case with sensitive stories like this, the whole truth will almost certainly remain an enigma.

CHAPTER 14:
GATEWAY BETWEEN WORLDS

THE OVERTOUN BRIDGE IS IN THE WESTERN PART OF DUNBARTONSHIRE, Scotland. It sits on an estate named Overtoun Farm before the White family purchased the land and built their mansion there. Built in the 1860s, it was apparent that they needed a bridge to connect the estate to its neighboring property for easier access. Hence, they constructed the Overtoun Bridge in 1895.

Unlike some of the other places we have discussed, the intriguing history of Overtoun Bridge involves a sacred site. An area referred to in Gaelic myth as a "thin place". A thin place is a place where the physical world and the spiritual world meet, a portal of sorts that allows spiritual beings to cross the boundary. In Irish mythology, a thin place is commonly found near water.

The waterfall and the gushing stream that flows under the bridge certainly fit that description.

An interesting fact about the bridge is that a dog jumps off the overpass at least once a year and plummets to its death.

Researchers have conducted studies on this phenomenon. While only approximately one dog per year has died since the 1960s, over 600 dogs have mysteriously jumped. These numbers are simply too staggering to be disregarded. Scientifically speaking, some have tried to explain these occurrences due to an odd scent present at the bridge. The theory presented was that the smell led the dogs to chase after the source, causing them to leap off the bridge onto the rocky shoals beneath. But no one has been able to prove that such a scent is present.

The presence of a thin place could answer the question. Some say dogs can sense the spiritual world. There many accounts where dogs have protected their masters from some unseen danger, or comfort people who have recently lost loved ones'. Dogs seem to sense things humans can't. There is an entire show dedicated to these occurrences on the Animal Planet entitled *The Haunted*.

When dogs come to Overtoun bridge, they might sense spirits as the two worlds collide, and whether joy or madness drives them over the edge, who can tell? There is also an idea that the supernatural pulls on the dogs. One Celtic holiday, Samhain, recognizes a period when the physical and spiritual worlds come closer together. Our modern-day Halloween originates from this ancient festival.

Another tragedy transpired at the bridge, contributes to its legend. In 1994, the bridge was the site of a dreadful crime. A couple named Kevin and Eileen Moy were visiting along with their baby boy Eoghan. Little did the wife know that her husband was about to commit a heinous act. According to the Scotland Herald, "As they stood at Overtoun Bridge near a Dumbarton beauty spot, Moy suddenly dropped the baby to the wooded banks of a river forty two feet below and then tried to throw himself over, but was dragged back by his screaming wife. Bystanders scrambled down the steep banks, where Eoghan lay fatally injured. He died in the hospital the next day."

Moy later stated that he believed he was the Anti-Christ and that his son was Satan. Therefore, to save the world from all the evil they would do, he had to kill his son and himself. Whether he strongly felt the other world and was trying to send his son back through the portal, no one can tell. Either way, the child's death and the man's attempted suicide are another theorized connection between the bridge and the spiritual world.

Overtoun Bridge is not the only thin place in the world. They exist all over the globe. For example, Aokigahara, also known as the Suicide Forest in Japan, is another mysterious place where around one hundred suicides occur every year. Perhaps in situations like these, people feel connected to the other world and cannot help but be drawn to it. Of course, you are free to visit places like these, but beware that their power may just come over you to do something that you will forever regret or pay for with your life.

CHAPTER 15:
SHAPESHIFTING

WITH THE POPULARITY OF SHOWS LIKE *THE X-FILES AND GHOST HUNTERS*, paranormal happenings have stepped into the spotlight. Did you know that many of the episodes of *The X-Files* were based on real events? In this chapter, our subject was the basis for an episode entitled "Irresistible". The man named Donnie Pfaster in the show is loosely based on the real serial killer Jeffrey Dahmer.

Jeffrey Dahmer grew up as the older of two brothers in a suburb of Milwaukee, Wisconsin. His childhood was not terrible, but there was constant fighting between his parents, and his mother suffered chronic illness. He was a quiet boy, but did well in school and had a few friends. Early on, there were some oddities about him. For example, he took to collecting dead bugs and animals, and sometimes his friends would help him pick up roadkill. As a young and curious boy, the behavior didn't seem troubling. However, this would only be the beginning of his fascination with death.

Things went downhill as he approached Junior High. Even at the tender age of fourteen, he developed a drinking problem, and this alcoholic reputation at school caused him to become an outcast. It was during this time that Dahmer discovered he was gay. He daydreamed about relationships with other men. Even this early, Dahmer admitted he felt the need to have complete dominance over his sexual partner. At the age of sixteen, he planned the attack on a jogger that he found attractive. Alas, he could not execute his plan, as the jogger wasn't out on the day that Dahmer lay in wait.

Things at home did not improve. The year he graduated from high school, his parents separated. The suddenly empty house became a convenient staging ground for Dahmer's first murder. He was eighteen. He brought a hitchhiker home, killed him, and then dissected and buried his body after sexually gratifying himself on the naked corpse. After graduation, he enlisted in the US Army, delaying his steps towards becoming a serial killer for nine more years. Even though he killed no one during his enlistment, a fellow officer reported being repeatedly raped by him.

When Dahmer returned from the Army, he lived with his grandmother, who resided in the same area that Dahmer grew up. At first, things seemed to go well, and he even attended church with her and did chores. However, this didn't last long. After being propositioned by a man while reading in a library, his old desires resurfaced, and he once again sought out sexual encounters. One thing led to another, and Dahmer once more ended up killing one of his partners. However, this first killing was not purposeful. Dahmer reports he woke up the next day after a night of mutual passion with another man, but found him lying dead in bed next to him with his chest crushed and blood everywhere. Dahmer claims he has no recollection of committing this crime, but it led to an increased appetite for blood.

In total, Dahmer ended up committing seventeen murders. Each death became more and more violent. He kept the skulls of his victims and even resorted to cannibalism. He ate all kinds of body parts of his victims and was known to serve human flesh to unsuspecting people. This earned him the nickname "Milwaukee Cannibal". At one point, he became fascinated with the idea of a sex slave. He tried to lobotomize several of his victims to keep them enslaved permanently, but he never succeeded, as his victims always died. When the police finally caught Dahmer, he was building an altar to himself out of the bones of the victims. When police arrested him, they found several skulls and other bones in his refrigerator and other preserved body parts he kept as trophies of his past killings.

Jeffrey Dahmer readily admitted to all the murders he was charged with and was sentenced to sixteen years to life. Ironically, Dahmer didn't last long in prison. He was beaten and killed by another inmate, cutting his sentence short.

But what does all this have to do with the paranormal? It doesn't seem like Dahmer's story could get any wilder, but it does. One of Dahmer's hostages survived, and the tales he told about his tormentor are genuinely terrifying. He claims Dahmer would change his form and turn into a hideous demon-like creature.

Shapeshifting has been part of legend and myth for millennia. Many old fairy tales talk about characters that can change their form into those of animals, usually done with the help of a deity. In Dahmer's case, the shapeshifting might be more complicated than that. The fact that the form he took was that of a demon begs the question: was Dahmer possessed?

The idea of possession has been around for as long as history. An evil spirit overcomes entirely ordinary people, then forces them to do genuinely hideous acts. If Dahmer were indeed possessed, this would certainly explain how a normal, healthy boy could grow up and be capable of all the unspeakable horrors of his crimes.

But can possession be proven? That problem is the reason why debates on the integrity of paranormal events go on and on. For anyone who first-handedly experience such horrors and lived to tell the tale, it is more than real.

CHAPTER 16:
THE BLACK-EYED CHILDREN

Cannock Chase is a pristine English district located in Staffordshire County. This twenty-six square mile area includes forests, large open fields, and old mines. Great Britain's national nature reserve designated Cannock Chase as a Site of Special Scientific Interest because of it contains diverse landscape and wildlife in such a concentrated area. Apart from boasting beautiful natural scenery, Cannock Chase is also home to a history of paranormal encounters spanning centuries. As a result, it is one of the hottest spots for supernatural activity in the United Kingdom.

Since as far back as the 1800s, people have reported a wide range of unexplained experiences, sightings, and confrontations. Over the years, some of the most prominent phenomena have included the notorious British big cats, which are purportedly mysterious felines about the size of a panther that are not indigenous to Britain. Others have claimed to see Bigfoot, UFOs, and even werewolves in the area. However, quite a few witnesses have touched upon one legend over the last few decades, which may be the most disturbing of them all—primarily because it has a solid story behind it.

With an uptick in activity during the 1980s, hikers and other wanderers reported bone-chilling sightings and direct encounters with odd little children who stalk the area around Cannock, especially the wooded areas. The accounts usually involve a small girl in a pale dress with deep, black eyes. At other times, reports include multiple children as part of a single incident, followed by unusual sounds such as giggling, children asking for help, or outright screaming.

Some of those interested in the case—professional paranormal investigators and curious individuals—have suggested that these sightings may be part of a dark chapter in Cannock Chase's history.

In the 1960s, several reports of abductions and murders of little girls began in the area. The horror started in 1964, when a cyclist found a nine-year-old girl barely holding onto life in the woods. The child had been raped, strangled, and left to die; which luckily didn't happen, thanks to the passersby. A little over a year later, two girls aged five and six, who had been missing for some time, were found dead in a ditch in Cannock Chase. Then, in the summer of 1967, a seven-year-old was found abused and murdered not too far away from where the previous two girls were discovered.

The murders had similarities, such as a stranger luring the girls into a car. But things soon turned when a girl escaped her abductor, and police connected the dots thanks to a witness of the attempted kidnapping. After one of the largest-scale criminal investigations and manhunts in the UK's history, the police apprehended Raymond Leslie Morris. Charging him with one murder and safely assuming the perpetrator was responsible for the rest of the crimes, they locked Raymond up until his death in March of 2014.

The ghostly sightings began roughly a decade after this tragic episode. Many believe them to be the trapped spirits of these poor children, claiming they haunt Cannock Chase to this day, lost in the woods.

A woman named Jane Massy described an encounter she had in the summer of 1985. Jane was spending a day outdoors with her friends in Cannock, enjoying nature for the day. Some time in the early evening hours, the group hung out, drinking beer and having a good time. Jane thought she heard the voice of what sounded like a frightened girl calling for help from somewhere nearby.

She asked, "Did you guys hear that?"

Her friends didn't know what she was talking about. Not wanting to embarrass herself anymore, Jane just brushed it off. But she heard it again. It sounded like a kid screaming. Even though it was odd to Jane, no one else heard it. She investigated and tried to determine where the cries were coming from. They sounded relatively close. She thought her search wouldn't be long, and was worried a child may be hurt or lost. Her search led her to a dirt road near a tree line. A little girl emerged from between two trees, wearing a white dress with blonde highlighted hair, and called for help. The girl didn't look hurt or in trouble. Jane thought she was possibly lost and afraid.

The child was holding her hands over her eyes. Jane was about five yards away, but as she approached the young girl, Jane immediately felt an empty dread fall in the pit of her stomach. The girl lowered her arms and pierced the woman with a horrifying gaze from two entirely black, soulless eyes.

> *"Her eyes had no white on them at all. They were purely black."*
>
> – Jane Massey

The girl stood there, saying nothing, and stared. The woman stepped back while keeping her eyes fixed on the little girl. Jane tripped over a log lying behind her and fell hard, severely injuring her arm. After a few minutes of rolling around in the dirt, holding her arm in pain, Jane sat up and looked where the little black-eyed girl was and found she was gone. Jane had an uneasy feeling, as if eyes were peering at her from every direction of the tree line. She got up and headed back.

The following day, Jane was released from the hospital with a cast around her arm. One of her friends took her home, and during the car ride the friend suggested reporting the incident to the police, to be safe.

Jane agreed, thinking maybe it was a missing child, and she possibly imagined her black eyes. The police came the following day to inquire about what she saw since it could be a case of a missing child, though there were no reports at the time. The police searched the same area soon enough but found no trace of the girl, and no news of a missing child ever came up.

Stories such as Jane's have become more common throughout the years. And like the Cannock Chase, sightings of black-eyed children have been reported all over the world. Coinciding with the death of Raymond Morris on March 11th, 2014 — of natural causes — an increasing number of sightings were reported from Cannock, indicating a possible return of the creepy children.

There have also been some photos and pieces of video footage captured over time. But, some are more extreme than others, a photo released in 2014, from a woman named Melissa Mason, showing two of her kids climbing a tree and what appears to be a ghost of a child on the right side of the picture. It certainly looks like a ghost. But with so many fakes nowadays, it's safe to assume this was anything but a prank.

A man who visited the Cannock captured video in 2014 which shows children's silhouettes appearing from the tree lines. Jeremy explained that the footage looked as though he could see small figures moving through the woods.

To prove he did not manipulate the video, he took it to a video forensic expert. The expert analyzed it and determined it to be genuine, showing no signs of tampering or alterations.

The footage is recorded in the almost absolute darkness of the Cannock Chase woods, with what seems to be the camera's light illuminating the trees only feet away, beyond which everything is pitch-black. Then, childlike figures seem to creep past them, further ahead in the woods, just beyond the light's range. The silhouettes appeared to be moving quickly, then disappearing into the darkness. Jeremy still doesn't know how the mysterious childlike figures can be seen so distinctly in the enveloping darkness.

Another woman named Mrs. Kelly was taking a stroll with her daughter down the Birches Valley. Their walk was suddenly interrupted by a scream from somewhere in the vicinity. She got her daughter and rushed to locate what she thought was a child in need of help. They couldn't find anybody, but upon stopping for a quick break, Mrs. Kelly clearly saw a small girl, whom she thought to be around ten. The child was holding her hands over her eyes.

The woman inquired if it was her who had been screaming, and whether she was okay. Then the girl lowered her arms and pierced the woman with a horrifying gaze from two entirely black eyes. Petrified, Mrs. Kelly took hold of her daughter, only to notice that the strange child had vanished.

While all these stories remain inconclusive, they all share similar details on the appearance and behavior of the black-eyed children. It is important to maintain a healthy dose of skepticism toward the reports. There is always a possibility the witnesses were hallucinating at the time of their alleged encounters. Whether these stories are real, one thing is certain: There's something bizarre going on in Cannock Chase.

CHAPTER 17:
THE CAROLYN STICKNEY EVP

URKY OLD PHOTOS, SPOKEN TESTIMONIES, AND AGE-OLD LEGENDS ARE, of course, not the only form of evidence that you can come across if you search for paranormal phenomena. In case it needs explanation, EVP stands for Electronic Voice Phenomena. Paranormal investigators, and other enthusiasts sometimes use this method in locations purported as hosting paranormal activity. It involves recording sounds with various devices and performing an in-depth analysis of the audio to search for peculiarities. Mostly, EVPs are recordings thought to contain sounds made by actual ghosts and other paranormal forces. Now and then, investigators pick up something quite fascinating.

Such is the case of Princess Carolyn Stickney and the supposed haunting of the Mount Washington Hotel, although "haunting" may not be the most appropriate word for what was discovered. Carolyn doesn't seem to be a malicious ghost, and the word haunting often carries a negative connotation. Most of the strange occurrences reported at the hotel usually boil down to flickering lights, alleged ghost appearances, unexplained sounds, or small objects disappearing. What she seems to be, however, is possibly one of the most convincing spirits ever documented. And this is because of one case involving an EVP, which we will cover soon enough.

A wealthy railroad industrialist by the name of Joseph Stickney masterminded the Mount Washington Hotel in New Hampshire in 1900. Around two years and a fortune later, the hotel officially opened. Joseph had put a lot of money and effort into constructing this masterpiece, but passed away only a year after its grand opening. Carolyn, the succeeding owner of the hotel, made some contributions of her own to the hotel over the next decade, building a new floor between the hotel's towers, a private dining room for her inner circle, and a chapel in memory of Joseph. She also had a large balcony installed overlooking the hotel's main dining room, from where she could observe the guests. There have been reports, over the years, of her apparition showing up on this balcony.

After a while, she remarried to a French prince, who referred to her as Princess Carolyn. She spent some time in France with her royal husband then returned to spend her last days in the hotel. She had her private apartment, now Room 314, into which she had her bed placed and where it remains to this day. As one may expect, this room is something of a hotspot for paranormal activity. There have been numerous reports of strange happenings there, including flickering lights and unusual noises. One story from a visiting couple described a woman sitting on the bed, fixing her hair.

Reports of paranormal activity by hotel employees began not long after Carolyn's death in 1936. Guests reported seeing her apparition in her favorite spots quite a few times, and a mysterious figure would show up in photographs of the staff after they developed them. Around this time, people at the hotel witnessed lights shutting on and off by themselves and even bathtubs mysteriously filling up.

But it was in February of 2008 when the most impressive paranormal evidence cropped up. Jason and Grant, two investigators from The Atlantic Paranormal Society (TAPS), decided to investigate the stories at the hotel. They were working as part of their *Ghost Hunters* show on Syfy. They conducted a thorough investigation of the Mt. Washington Hotel, and they focused mainly on the infamous Room 314. The two Ghost Hunters confirmed hearing and recorded mysterious steps throughout the hotel, which they couldn't identify the source.

However, this was child's play compared to what they caught on tape in the Princess' old quarters in Room 314. It was here where they tried to elicit paranormal activity and establish contact with the supposed ghost by asking her questions. No one could have predicted the mysterious outcome as the exclusively male crew received answers in a female voice. The voice was not clear, but it was almost entirely audible, and what was said could be discerned with almost complete confidence.

At first, the footage shows men standing and observing the room, apparently commenting on the interior and discussing the case. Amid them talking, the recording devices picked up what appeared to be a female voice speaking rapidly. It occurred again as they discussed the Princess's old bed. After that, the investigators attempted to talk to the ghost directly.

One of the men whispered, "Princess, are you in here?"

The same muffled voice, sounding like it was coming from under the water, responded barely audibly. It seemed to say, "Hello. Is there someone there?"

The man repeated his question and asked her to confirm that she was in the room. Things got creepy at that point, as she responds once again, this time more clearly. Most would agree that she said, "Of course I'm in here. Where are you?" Still, the voice was not entirely audible, but it was improving.

The team tried to get her to give a physical sign by moving an object or doing something of the sort. All their questions were met with the same answer, though. "Of course, I'm in here. Where are you?" she kept asking.

The audio recording and video footage were, of course, featured on the *Ghost Hunters* episode, and are also available on the internet for anybody to see. In the show, the Ghost Hunters shared their audio recordings with the head of security at the hotel, Fred Hollis, and filmed his reaction. The man reacted at the very first moment when the female voice makes herself known. He said that he could clearly understand what she said, and his reaction seemed to be one of genuine but controlled fascination.

Everybody who watches the footage can judge for themselves, though.

Hollis explained he had his own strange experiences at the hotel in the past, such as mysterious sounds. These peculiar incidents he witnessed were usually very subtle, just enough to arouse suspicion, but not sufficient for a rational man to draw a definite conclusion. At the times when these "encounters" happened, Hollis was unsure of what he heard, if anything at all, so he didn't pay much mind to them. However, he said the recordings presented to him by the *Ghost Hunters* crew were absolutely in line with his experiences. After hearing it, he felt he had confirmation that he had indeed been hearing mysterious sounds around the hotel.

Some may find this case particularly fascinating because the ghost itself differs greatly from what you would usually expect, based on most of the stories of hauntings in popular culture. Princess Carolyn's life wasn't that of tragedy, and neither was her death. On the contrary, she lived a fulfilled life, ran the hotel until her very end, and passed away naturally in a place she loved. Could this be the reason that her supposed ghost appears to be pleasant, and could it be possible for a trapped soul wandering the physical world to even be friendly?

The recording differs so much from what many expect from a haunting, it's almost as if the recording lets us see into the "psyche" of a spirit. More so than just being friendly, Carolyn—if it actually is her in the recording—seems confused and lost. Most of us would usually think of a ghost as malicious or even dangerous, something in control over its reality. In contrast, we are the ones who are confused, petrified, and helpless.

Although hearing a ghostly voice speaking in a haunted place might be terrifying, once you think about this recording, things take on a whole new light. The way that the Princess keeps asking if someone is there and simply saying hello gives us the impression of someone who doesn't know what exactly is going on. She doesn't want to throw things around, cut the phone lines, terrify anybody, or make the walls bleed. Instead, Carolyn appears to be trying to establish communication, just like the *Ghost Hunters* were doing. And if she responded with, "Of course I'm here," then that implies that in her world or plane of existence, there is no doubt as to what she is and what she's doing. It's almost as if the *Ghost Hunters* themselves are the intruders, disturbing her peace, and not the other way around. Maybe the living souls that visit the hotel appear as ghosts to Carolyn, leaving her just as confused as we would be upon seeing or hearing an apparition.

We'd never think that we would be the ones who must explain ourselves if we ran into a ghost. However, apart from Carolyn being perplexed by the investigators' questioning of her presence, the rest of the exchange still implies a dose of confusion from the ghost's point of view.

There is an array of posts on forums and websites about ghosts on the internet. Some people on those forums say we exist simultaneously in two parallel realms of existence with the spirits. Sometimes, these realms flow into each other in something of an inter-dimensional glitch, if you will. When this overlap occurs, ghosts stumble into our realm by accident, resulting in all kinds of paranormal phenomena for the witnesses. But maybe we can accidentally slip into the spiritual world just the same. Perhaps ghosts are not even aware of their death, and they continue living as if nothing happened, without even knowing that they have transcended into a new reality in what appears to be their regular life. Could it be that if a living, mortal soul were to wander beyond their three-dimensional world, those who occupy the beyond might be just as shocked as we are when we perceive the supposed ghosts?

Furthermore, the spirit of the late Carolyn may be trapped in time in a way that we can't even fathom, where it flows in a non-linear way or freezes completely. So, her perception of time may be entirely different from ours, leading to a lot of confusion.

Whatever the case may be, and whether the recordings are valid proof of paranormal activity, we can hardly draw any definitive conclusions, even after watching the episode and hearing the uncanny recording for ourselves. There are a few things we can do, though. First, we can speculate on what this may or may not prove and what it tells us about the paranormal. Alternatively, we can stay at the Mount Washington Hotel, which continues to be a prosperous institution to this day. They offer an authentic vintage experience of luxury and incredible scenery, as well as the possibility to have your paranormal encounter. After all, Carolyn's shenanigans, as well as other reported ghostly activity, are not kept secret. The hotel doesn't hide this peculiar quirk in their luxury accommodations.

CHAPTER 18:
THE GOLDFIELD HOTEL

THERE HAVE BEEN MANY ALLEGED ELECTRONIC VOICE PHENOMENA OVER THE YEARS, and going over all of them would be quite a tedious feat. After all, many of the recordings are distorted, dim, or not particularly awe-inspiring. Nevertheless, there may be only a few EVPs that come close to the Princess of Mt. Washington Hotel. The recording from the old Goldfield Hotel is one of them. Arguably, it is even more bewildering than Princess Carolyn, especially considering some of the other stories, events, and investigative experiences in Goldfield Hotel, before and long after its closure in 1945.

The Goldfield Hotel is a dilapidated and allegedly haunted building in a small, stagnating town of Goldfield in Nevada. The history of this town begins in 1902 with the discovery of gold in the area, which sparked an influx of people and quickly got the town established. It wasn't long until the city became very active and prosperous due to the productive mining industry around it. Soon, it became the largest city in the state and was home to some 35,000 people at its peak.

However, not even a decade passed until the resources depleted in the mines. The dried-up mine caused many of the townsfolk to move on and take the gold rush elsewhere. As the gold mining industry declined, the town devolved, ultimately using up all the gold ore. Then a terrible fire hit the town in the 1920s, decreasing the population amounting to five hundred people.

The Goldfield Hotel itself was officially opened in 1908 as quite a luxurious place, boasting four stories and 154 rooms, fully equipped with the necessary utilities. The hotel became successful quickly, mainly because it drew in guests from the upper classes, particularly those who came through looking to invest or start their gold mining ventures.

One such man was a wealthy mining industrialist named George Winfield, who bought the hotel as part of his hotel entrepreneurship side-path. His investment made him quite a lot of money, adding to his already enormous wealth.

Winfield is allegedly also one ghost who still haunts the historic hotel, along with the spirit of a woman named Elizabeth. According to some controversial legends, the two had known each other rather well when they were still among the living. In addition, there have been numerous reports of other ghosts wandering the building, such as children and at least two other people who allegedly committed suicide in the hotel. The tale of Winfield and Elizabeth, though, is particularly dark.

Elizabeth is said to have been a prostitute around the 1920s and 1930s, with George Winfield as her regular customer. As the story suggests, misfortune struck when Elizabeth found out she was pregnant and told Winfield he was the father, urging him to leave his wife and marry her instead. George tried to keep her away, giving her money to survive independently and keeping the pregnancy quiet. He was hoping to avoid complications that could harm him, as he was a prominent and influential individual in Nevada. However, his plan didn't work for very long, as Elizabeth was relentless in her demands for justice and ultimately returned to him.

Things took a dark turn here as Elizabeth died in the 1930s. It's not known how, but people believe it happened in one of two ways. Some suggest she died in childbirth, but others have alleged that Winfield murdered her in cold blood. The theory is that he tied Elizabeth to a radiator in his private Room 109 at the hotel. He kept her there until she was about to give birth. He fed her and provided her with water to keep her alive. According to different versions of the story, she either died in the room when it came time to birth their child, or Winfield murdered her after the fact. He allegedly then took the baby to the basement and threw it down one of the mine shafts underneath the hotel.

Whether or not these events transpired as told by the legends is still debated to this day. But reports of their ghosts and other paranormal activity at the hotel have been numerous. As a result, the hotel is widely known as a haunted place, attracting many visitors and enthusiasts. Unfortunately, this enthusiasm is one reason efforts to renovate have stagnated, because of trespassing and vandalism.

Among the visitors was a crew from *Ghost Adventures*, who came to investigate the reports on multiple occasions. In 2008, the *Ghost Adventures* show organized a well-documented, videotaped investigation of the premises, featured later. This event is one of the most incredible paranormal footage, and it's well-known among paranormal circles. The team was in the basement, looking for anything strange to record with their cameras. First, they go around in the darkness, asking for any ghosts to come out. Just moments after that, a brick lifts off and flies across the room, smashing against the wall with a terrifying crash. The situation gets hectic quickly, and the investigators scramble in the darkness. At this time, what sounds like children's voices can be heard periodically from somewhere around them. Of course, it didn't take long for the team to disappear from the premises, and this EVP was among the last things recorded during this particular excursion by the Ghost Adventures.

However, this wasn't even close to the best EVP recording obtained at the Goldfield Hotel. This shocker came sometime later when the *Ghost Adventures* returned once again. This time, however, they had Mark and Debby Constantino with them. This couple was in the same line of work, but they were reasonably skeptical of both the hotel and the footage previously presented by Ghost Adventures. The Constantinos, who led the investigation, brought a news crew from the KTVN with cameras, ready to capture all the evidence right on television.

The Constantinos went around for a while, recording, asking for any sign from the ghosts, if they were present. In the piece, Debby uses a sound recorder as she tries to communicate. They hear nothing at first, and the cameras capture nothing. However, she then tries a different approach. Debby thought perhaps they couldn't hear the EVPs with their ears so she asked the ghost, "Can you at least tell me, in the recorder, if you did it?" — referring to the incident with the brick.

Then, they played back what the recorder picked up and were shocked to hear a response. What resembled a female voice said, "Thank you, but we've done it." The words sounded slightly cut up, and there was static. The investigators didn't stop there. They managed to engage the alleged ghost once again, using the same method.

The team asked another question and continued to inquire about the brick. The voice responded again with, "Didn't mean to hurt anybody." This second response was clearer than the first one. Matters of authenticity aside, the recorded, spoken word is next to irrefutable in the audio. Still, there haven't been many claims against the recordings as being faked. Likewise, there isn't any evidence exposing the audio as being genuine either.

Another fact perhaps worth mentioning is that the Constantino couple were found dead in an apartment in 2015, ruled a murder-suicide perpetrated by Mark in a case of domestic violence gone wrong. It's unclear what exactly led to this tragedy, but the couple had a strained relationship for a while and was going through a range of other personal problems in their lives.

As for our mystery voice in the Goldfield Hotel, it remains an enigma. If there truly is a spirit at work on the premises, it's unclear if is the restless soul of Elizabeth or someone else. Reports describe her apparition as a sad, heart-broken lady who hopelessly stalks the hallways searching for her child. As for Winfield, some witnesses have alleged that they would run into traces of mysterious cigar smoke that seems to emit from no natural source. Experts indicate that this could be the residue of his spirit, as it traverses his old hotel, smoking the cigars he enjoyed in life just the same. There are problems with the legend of these two departed, though, and inconsistencies between different versions. Winfield didn't remain the owner of the hotel until the very end. Instead, it was sold to another man not long after the town began to deteriorate. There are conflicting accounts of when exactly Elizabeth died and if Winfield had even been the owner when it happened.

Details of such stories, which span decades and were spread mostly by word of mouth, often become muddled and result in disarray in the story. However, that isn't to say there isn't a fine thread of truth that snakes its way through the different versions and recollections, especially when so much strange activity is reported by so many people who can't explain just what they experienced. Combined with the startling, documented evidence, all of this makes for an unusual place that continues to garner much attention as people thirsty for answers pass through the hotel in search of the truth.

CHAPTER 19:
X-RAY VISION

PARANORMAL ACTIVITY, WHILE FRIGHTENING, CAN ALSO BE QUITE REWARDING. Stan Lee, who helped create famous comic book heroes such as The Avengers and The Amazing Spider-Man, came out with a television show that broadcasts men and women's superhuman or paranormal abilities all over the world entitled *Stan Lee's Superhumans*. These wide-ranged paranormal abilities covered everything from superhuman strength to superhuman mental acuity. People featured on this show include Salim Haini, known for his incredible ability to eat anything, Zamora the Torture King, who can skewer himself without feeling any pain whatsoever, and Miroslaw Magola, a man with telekinetic abilities.

Some of these abilities may seem more valuable than others. But imagine if you had a skill that could truly help others? Would you use your power? Using this talent is the choice that Natasha Demkina faces every day.

Natasha was born in 1987 in Saransk, Mordovia. While her life appeared to be completely normal at the start, her parents soon took notice of a unique ability that set her apart, a skill that lay in her vision. One day Natasha walked into the room and realized her ability to see her mother's organs, as though she had x-ray vision. However, unlike with an x-ray, Natasha could see each organ in full living color and movement. Imagine how the wealth of information generated by all the additional detail of Natasha's vision could aid doctors in the accuracy of their diagnosis. Once her mother had told others of her abilities, residents frequently dropped by to receive prognoses from the girl with the unusual ability.

Natasha spent a lot of time in Russia helping doctors at the children's hospital in Saransk with quite a bit of success. Among her accurate 'readings', Natasha could see the precise location of an ulcer in one of the doctor's stomachs. She could also differentiate benign cysts from harmful material. A word about her unique gift inevitably spread worldwide, and she was soon invited to England, the United States, and then Japan to talk about and prove her abilities. The test in New York City, however, did not put Natasha in a good light. Her success rate only seemed to be at a little under 60%. Because of these results, the scientific community legitimately discredited Natasha. It appeared to the critics she was merely guessing, and perhaps had a passing familiarity with medicine allowing her to make some accurate guesses and was able to 'read' people to diagnose them.

Meanwhile, other experts attempted to discredit the criticisms. However, the test in Tokyo, Japan, went much smoother than the test administered in the United States, finally making a valid case for the authenticity of her skills. As Natasha's superhuman ability is only in her vision and not her capacity to diagnose, she is currently studying medicine at Semashkow's Moscow Medical University. Hopefully, this will help her fine-tune her skills and save many lives in the future.

There you have it! We have gone through some intriguing, if not gruesome, and horrifying true-to-life events. Real mysteries often cannot be logically explained. Not all the paranormal is evil, and not all evil acts stem from the paranormal — assuming either exist at all. Faced with the claims, it is within ourselves to choose what to believe in and what we deny.

CONCLUSION

I HOPE YOU HAVE ENJOYED THESE BAFFLING AND SHOCKING STORIES dealing with paranormal activities worldwide. These hard-to-believe stories continually challenge us to keep an open mind. Being aware, though, may one day save your soul.

Most of the events presented above begin and end with no sense of logic.

While these stories may seem improbable, the claims might make you wonder... what if? Legends and myths have come to be for a reason. And each account may have the tiniest truth to it. But the truth will eventually reveal itself.

Understanding these stories might help you better understand the legends and myths that permeate so many cultures in the world. Remember that almost every story has a seed of truth in it—no matter how far-fetched it may seem.

Ghosts and spirits do not discriminate in their activity by class or area of the world, even though some places seem to have more paranormal activity than others. People from all walks of life and all social levels have had their run-ins with hauntings, ghostly apparitions, and humans with paranormal abilities. The wealthiest people, such as Sarah Winchester, to the most neglected soul, such as Richard Ramirez, may relate to the spiritual world, and are equally susceptible to hauntings and other ghostly activities.

Chances are, you will have your run-in at some point in your life. But, just as groups exist for those who believe in extraterrestrial life, you can also find a support group if you end up dealing with a disturbing spiritual experience. Just remember, you are not alone.

GHOST
STORIES

A COLLECTION OF THE WORLD'S MOST
HAUNTED LOCATIONS AND PARANORMAL
ENCOUNTERS

VOL II

H.J. TIDY

INTRODUCTION

THERE IS NOTHING MORE INTERESTING THAN A GOOD ghost story. For generations, we have gathered around campfires, huddled at sleepovers, and whispered in cemeteries about the stories we have heard, especially those which have terrified us. So many of us are addicted to the rush of a good horror tale, and we find spooky stories the most fascinating. However, many feel the best tales told are the true ones, and that is what this book is about. Exploring the truth behind famous myths and legends is just as interesting as the fictional — and sometimes even scarier.

It is infinitely more engaging to hear about first-hand accounts of the paranormal, especially when multiple people have experienced the same events. It is also more believable, as the stories become part of supernatural lore and history. By drawing on the facts of the stories, it is easy to discern what is fact and fiction and further explore the world of the supernatural.

The stories in this book will explore distinct narratives, all of which have several eyewitnesses who experienced the same ordeals. While it was often a primary individual who was involved with the sighting, every story has other witnesses to corroborate what the primary individual has experienced.

Some stories are gruesome, while others are psychologically terrifying. One of the most intriguing parts is that they happened to real-life people, some of whom even lived to tell the tale themselves. This book is not here to convince you of the supernatural or even make you believe the stories, but to entertain with the real-life accounts of these people. You may even change your mind about what you believe.

In this book, eight distinct and different accounts of the paranormal will be told, making for some of the spookiest stories in North America. Stories filled with witnesses, and some even with physical evidence; each one engaging in its own way. So please join me as I delve once again into the world of haunted locations, paranormal experiences, and demonic possessions.

CHAPTER 1:
AMERICA'S GREATEST GHOST STORY

STORIES OF WITCHES, THE SUPERNATURAL, AND GHOSTS HAVE EXISTED FOR CENTURIES. Even before the advent of written language, people whispered these tales to one another. They traveled far and wide. Interest in the supernatural is among the oldest aspects of human society.

For the greatest ghost story in American history, we need only cast our minds back to the 1800s, where the story of the Bell Witch began. This supernatural occurrence originates in the town of Adams, Tennessee, and is entrenched in Southern mystical history.

Since tales of this apparition began, many have believed in its existence. Countless individuals have come forward with their experiences, and feel they have proof that she exists.

There is a mystery surrounding who the Bell Witch is. There are many theories. However, it is difficult to distinguish fact from fiction. It is particularly tricky as this happened so many years ago, and those who went through these experiences are long gone.

Like with any supernatural story, some are dubious of how legitimate these eyewitness accounts are. Some have attempted to debunk the narrative and prove that it is nothing more than folklore. It is difficult to have the full picture of what is true and what is hearsay. As always, I am not here to convince you of what to believe. I simply want to tell you the story of the Bell Witch.

How much you believe is up to you.

Note: This story briefly mentions sexual assault in the third section. Reader discretion is advised.

The Legend of The Bell Witch

This legend begins with the Bell Family, who moved to Tennessee in 1804. They lived on a farm in Robertson County and experienced many trials and triumphs in their time together. While one of their children died at a young age, the rest flourished, marrying and having children of their own. Zadok Bell became a prominent lawyer and Thomas Gunn, a successful farmer (Tennessee State Library and Archives, n.d.). The women of the family married well, which was very important at the time. Unfortunately, the family also experienced the horrors of being haunted by a vengeful spirit.

The history of the Bell Witch herself began in the family home in 1817. The Bells noticed strange phenomenon around the house and farm, which they could not find the source of. They saw strange animals roaming the area and heard unexplained noises coming from different parts of the house. It soon became apparent to them that a supernatural entity was making itself known.

They eventually made contact with this ghost, who revealed herself to be an evil entity sent to torture the family. Their neighbor, Kate Bates (sometimes referred to as Kate Batts), was the one who purportedly performed some sort of dark magic as retribution for a family feud.

The first historical documentation that references the existence of the Bell Witch comes from the year 1820, in the form of a journal entry. This was written by John R. Bell, a military officer who stopped by the residence one night for dinner. While there, the family told him about what was happening to them. He wrote of the daughter's experience, stating, "A voice accompanies her, which says she should marry a man, a neighbor–thousands of persons have visited her to hear this voice." (Fitzhugh, 2020).

There is even a story of President Andrew Jackson, who allegedly stayed at the property for just one night. His plan was to remain there longer, but he left after one night from the fear he experienced. He later said, "I vow I would rather fight the entire British Army single-handed than face this witch again." (White, 2004).

Who Was the Bell Witch?

The prevailing theory of the witch's identity supports the Bell family's story that the entity was, in fact, sent by Kate Bates. Some believe this relates to a woman who lived in a nearby town that quarreled with John Bell, the Bell family patriarch, and cursed them with dark magic by summoning a spirit to their house. The dispute was over land, and Kate felt as though John Bell was attempting to cheat her while making a deal. Kate was reportedly often heard saying that she would get even with John, and spoke of this even on her deathbed.

Some also believe John murdered Kate due to the torment she forced his family to endure. Others posit the idea John murdered Kate first, and then she came back to punish the family.

It's difficult to know what is true and what isn't. The records kept in the 1800s are not clear. Some have been lost; others never existed. Perhaps we will never know what really went on between Kate and the Bells, though that might be why the story is so intriguing.

Where is the Bell Witch Now?

Following John Bell's death in 1820, a mere three years after the haunting began, the sightings of the witch became few and far between. In fact, the spirit seemingly disappeared for seven years. The children who remained on the property claim that she came back in 1827, behaving exactly as she had before. She vanished once again and did not reappear until 1935, when the entity returned to haunt descendants of the Bell family (Tennessee State Library and Archives, n.d.).

In the last few decades, people have claimed to have seen the witch at the former Bell home. The sightings are rare. However, those who witness this supernatural being are often terrified for their lives. This is no peaceful spirit; this is something born of dark magic that intends to frighten and harm the living.

Despite the reduced sightings in recent years, the story of the Bell Witch still fascinates people. Movies such as *An American Haunting* and *Bell Witch Haunting* have been made based on the narrative, and people still research the history, hoping to find an answer to what really happened.

While the history of this haunting tale is interesting, the events of the haunting are absolutely shocking.

Disturbing Encounters

Since her first appearance in 1817, the Bell Witch has made herself known to many people. This spirit torments those who encounter her and instills fear into the hearts of all who visit the former Bell family home. Even though some seek her out, they acknowledge that seeing her is a terrifying prospect.

The Bell Family

It only makes sense to tell the story of the Bell family's encounters first. After all, they are the first ones to have ever encountered her and seemingly the reason she was summoned in the first place. And, of course, the entity was named after them.

As mentioned before, the first supernatural sightings on the property involved strange animals roaming the farm. The family first saw something they assumed was a rabbit. However, upon closer inspection, they found something much larger and stranger. They likened it to some sort of hybrid of a rabbit and a large dog (Fitzhugh, 2013).

Strangely enough, it was John Bell's daughter, Betsy, who was the prime target of the haunting. It was Betsy that John R. Bell referenced in his journal entry, and it was her story that garnered the most attention. At the time of the witch's appearance, Betsy was madly in love with her betrothed, a man named was Gardener. The pair planned to marry as soon as possible, and by all accounts, the family and community were happy with this marriage. There was support for them to be together, and they loved one another very much.

However, this seemed to anger the witch greatly, and she set her sights on ensuring this union did not take place. She began by whispering to Betsy at all hours that she was not to marry Joshua. At first, this was harmless, and she simply ignored it. Then, the spirit became violent. The witch endlessly taunted her and physically abused her. Betsy was battered and bruised from these episodes. Wherever Betsy and Joshua went, the entity followed. It hunted them mercilessly. Eventually, this all became too much for Betsy, and she called the engagement off.

In addition to the mystery of why the witch was so angered by the presence of Joshua Gardener in Betsy's life, there was also another suitor vying for her hand. His name was Professor Richard Powell, who had been Betsy and Joshua's school teacher. He was eleven years older than her and was secretly married to another woman. Some wonder if the witch thought he would be a better match for young Betsy. If this was the case, she got exactly what she wanted. Betsy married Richard and they moved to Mississippi. For Betsy, this was the end of her torment.

The family also experienced the classic signs of a haunting. There were never-ending banging and clunking sounds with no explanation, and beds in the house were pulled apart. Sounds rattled against the windows and walls for hours on end, and the Bells were driven mad by the never-ending ruckus. The entire house shook at times. Some family members, like Betsy, were physically harmed. They would be bitten, pinched, and have their hair pulled. Sometimes, these attacks went on for hours.

Lucy Bell was the only family member who was treated kindly by the witch. The entity would sing to her when she was in the shower and would care for her when she was sick. There seems to be no reason why Betsy endured so much and Lucy was spared, though how could we possibly make sense of a witch's thought process.

It is also speculated the witch was the cause of John's death. He was gradually poisoned, which led to his passing. Many believe that the slow and painful circumstances were the result of dark magic.

William Porter

One of the more famous stories of the witch's interactions with another human is the tale of William Porter. He was a family friend of the Bells who lived only a short distance from their farm. William and the spirit became well acquainted, and he had no reason to fear her. He referred to her by her name, Kate, and he feared no harm from her. The witch, however, eventually struck. One freezing night, Kate asked to lie in William's bed. He heard her say she wanted "to spend the night with him and keep him warm" (Wick, 1987). William told her that if she wanted to sleep in his bed, she needed to behave herself, and Kate agreed to these terms. She did not keep her word.

That night, while William was sleeping, Kate pulled the covers from off him, exposing his body. He awoke to her crawling closer and closer to him. As this was happening, he had an idea. Rather than panicking and forcing her away, William moved to grab the spirit and wrap her in the bedsheets she was on top of. He then ran to throw her into the fire, hoping to burn her. Unfortunately, he was unsuccessful. William claimed that as he approached the fire, the weight of the entity got heavier and heavier, and that a horrible smell came from the bedsheets (Wick, 1987). He had to drop the witch and run for his life into the freezing outdoors. The legend goes that Kate never asked to spend the night with anyone ever again. This story is so well-known that one of the most famous illustrations of the witch is of William Porter attempting to burn her. It was drawn in 1894, many years after the incident, which shows just how important this event was to the lore of the Bell Witch.

Enslaved Persons

The Bell Witch famously had a vendetta against the enslaved persons at the Bell family property and tormented them relentlessly. She would not only taunt them at all times, but would often physically hurt the men and women at the farm. The witch had her sights set specifically on one enslaved person named Dean, who needed to carry protection with him to fight her off. He claimed that the spirit did not come to him in her human form, but rather as an animal. When this happened, she appeared as either a wolf or a dog; sometimes it had two heads, sometimes none at all (Tennessee State Library and Archives, n.d.).

There is no reason why the witch would go after these people. Some have proposed the idea that she was a bigot, though once again, there is no way of knowing.

Robert L. and The Shakers

In 1988, Robert L. and his band, The Shakers, were recording a song about the Bell Witch. It was titled "Living in the Shadow of a Spirit" and was born from Robert's childhood fascination with the legend of the entity. It became a four-song EP, as a single tune could not hold the entire story of this myth.

Robert visited the property many times with many people to gain knowledge about what the location was like. There was a cave nearby where townspeople often spotted the witch, and Robert thought this would be a great place to capture just how the people of the 1800s were feeling during her most active years. One such visit was with his girlfriend on a beautiful day. While in the cave, she turned and asked him if he could hear a noise. It was the sound of a woman singing at the far end of the cave. It was an ethereal sound. After listening to the noise for a while, Robert says the sound began to affect him physically. "It was an eerie sound that made us weak in the knees and it went on for a couple of minutes" (Fitzhugh, 2013). This was the only supernatural experience he had in the cave, but it was enough to spook him.

The Filming of The Bell Witch Haunting

When filming *The Bell Witch Haunting* movie in 2003, the crew of the film had quite a few experiences they recall as being quite strange. Ric White, the director, recounted hearing a strange voice while in the same cave that Robert L. had visited. He was

Ghost Stories Vol I & II

there with a writer for the movie, exploring in silence when they both heard a voice saying, "What are you doing here?" (Fitzhugh, 2013). They looked for the source of the noise but could not find the person who had spoken to them.

After filming and editing the movie, there was another incident. The office where the completed movie was stored spontaneously caught on fire. The origin of the fire was a fax machine that had been in the office the entire time. The team used it often and normally left it on while they weren't there. By all accounts, there was nothing wrong with it. Why it burst into flames was a complete mystery.

Luckily, Ric had a copy of the film at his home and was able to re-edit the footage there. While working, strange occurrences occurred in the house that he had never experienced before. The home became filled with a peculiar smell, he heard unexplained noises, and often had a strange feeling while working on the movie. He also had issues with technology. His cell phone malfunctioned, and his computer broke three times. Ric had it repaired time and time again, setting his work back a substantial amount (Fitzhugh, 2013). In his opinion, it was like the witch didn't like the way they were telling her story.

Ric also notes that several of their filming locations experienced fires in the months after the film crew had been there, including the church in town and the home of the Bell Witch Museum's curator. Unfortunately, she died in the blaze at the front door; it was clear she was trying to escape. Ric says that three unexplained fires in one year, connected only by this story, must be more than a coincidence. He is sure they had something to do with the Bell Witch.

A few years after the movie was released, producer Linda Thornton returned to the cave with a group of people. When she separated from the group to go back to her car, she heard a voice calling, "Linda! Linda!" (Fitzhugh, 2013). She assumed it was someone from the group trying to freak her out, but when she turned around, there was nobody near her. She then experienced an unnerving feeling that something was very wrong, and was left numb from the entire occurrence.

An Anonymous Source

In 1998, a witness who desires to stay anonymous experienced a sighting of the Bell Witch — though this story differs slightly from others. This person and three friends visited the property, inspired by curiosity about the legend. This person spent many years reading about the entity, and desired to see for themselves what all the fuss was about. They went to the farmhouse and found out it was closed. They then went to the clearing behind the property. There, they heard what they described as the strangest noise of their lives. The sound was so odd, this person attributed it to paranormal hounds roaming the property and stalking enslaved people from the 1800s. This person led the group as they walked into the field. That night, there was a full moon that illuminated the entire clearing. This person got a little in front of their friends when suddenly, the entire area went pitch black. It was like someone extinguished the light of the moon. They turned around and told their friends they would not go any further. Something was definitely wrong. No good would come from them continuing their exploration.

Debunking and Skeptics

Skeptics have had centuries to debunk and speculate on the true story of the Bell Witch. Unlike many other tales of hauntings, people have written scientific papers to explain the occurrences. Hours of research have gone into disproving the stories of those who believe in her legend, and some of the evidence is quite compelling.

A popular theory is that Betsy Bell's husband, Richard Powell, was behind a lot of the strange occurrences. He was so smitten with his former student that he was hellbent on making sure she didn't marry her sweetheart, Joshua. This was the reason he began an all-out campaign to ensure that their union never took place. Using "pranks, tricks, and with the help of several accomplices, it is theorized that Powell created all of the 'effects' of the ghost to scare Gardner away" (Wagner, 2017).

However, this theory does not explain the strange physical attacks others experienced, including Dean and Betsy's siblings. Richard had no motive to hurt or terrorize others.

Another theory is that this was a case of "the poltergeist-faking syndrome" where a child causes mischief (Kreidler, 2014). It does, however, seem hard to believe that a child could cause all these disturbances.

Dr. Meagan Mann, an assistant professor of chemistry at Austin Peay State University, decided to view the stories of the Bell Witch through a scientific lens. She began by looking into the Bell family and the records of people who lived in Adams at the time. She explored the circumstances around John Bell's death, which she explains to be the result of arsenic poisoning (Nixon, 2017). This caused strange twitching in his face, which many at the time thought resulted from dark magic, but could have been a side effect of the poison. She didn't acknowledge the remainder of the hauntings, but felt that she successfully disproved the notion that a witch murdered him.

A local psychic corroborates this theory, claiming she knows what happened to John Bell, sayings, "A slave killed John Bell, poisoning him because he could not protect Betsy, then eleven, from her father who was sexually abusing her" (Young, 2015). This could be the reason Betsy was so tormented during this time. Perhaps her young mind could not process the abuse she was experiencing, and she imagined the paranormal experience instead.

None of these theories cover all the circumstances, nor do they successfully explain away each incident; however, it is enough for many skeptics to believe that all of this is rumor and mythical storytelling.

The Bell Witch

Both the mythical and historical sides of the Bell Witch story are truly fascinating. No matter one's stance on the paranormal, learning about such a supernatural legend can be intriguing.

The farm is now open to visitors who hope to have a run-in with the witch. Though this might terrify some to their core, thrill-seekers and those inquisitive about the supernatural are determined to see this powerful entity. You can still visit the home, the farm, and the cave where the witch is thought to live. There are tours run by paranormal experts and those acquainted with the story of the Bell family. This is a popular place to visit when passing through Adams, Tennessee, and is an integral part of Southern mythology.

Whether you believe the various terrifying stories or are sure there is no way something like this could exist, it can be an incredibly engaging story. Many find the history behind the narrative to be particularly captivating, and learning all about the Bell family gives a great insight into life in nineteenth century America.

CHAPTER 2:
THE TRAGIC CASE AND HAUNTING OF THE LOS FELIZ MANSION

THE TRAGIC CASE OF THE LOS FELIZ MANSION IS ONE OF THE MOST FAMOUS true-crime stories of the twentieth century. Every true-crime podcast and television show in America has explored it, reaching a worldwide audience who have become obsessed with what happened. The property has become a tourist destination for true-crime afficionados, amassing as much popularity as the site of the Black Dahlia Murder and OJ Simpson's Brentwood home, both of which are also in Los Angeles. This story also had paranormal aspects which cannot be ignored.

This story begins with a family. Harold Perelson was a renowned cardiothoracic surgeon. His wife Lillian, was described as a caring mother and loving wife. They had three children: Judye, Joel, and Debbie.

At 4:30 am on December 6th, 1959, the doctor murdered one of his family members and brutally bludgeoned another, then ingested pills to end his own life. Since then, their home—dubbed the Los Feliz Mansion or the Los Feliz Murder House—has never been the same. So, who was this family, and why did this happen? What paranormal activity has there been in the house since, and what is happening in the mansion now?

Who Were the Perelsons?

By all accounts, the Perelsons were an average family. Lillian and Harold welcomed their first child, Judye, in 1941. Five years later, their son Joel was born. In 1948, they had their final child, Debbie. People who knew them, who babysat for them and came to dinners, are still baffled as to why this crime occurred.

Doctor Harold Perelson was not only a renowned surgeon, but he was also a well-respected keynote speaker at many medical conferences across the United States. He gained even further notoriety for inventing a new type of syringe. A child of Eastern European immigrants, he worked hard and was at the top of his professional career. He appeared to be a loving father, outwardly portraying a great relationship with his children and a healthy relationship with his wife.

In the early 1950s, the family moved to 2475 Glendower Place, a Spanish Revival-style house so large it was considered a mansion. The real-estate listing at the time boasted twelve rooms, spectacular views, and stunning gardens. It had a tiled entryway and a stairway that led to the living room, dining room, kitchen, breakfast room, den, and a beautiful glass conservatory. The second floor had four bedrooms and three bathrooms, as well as a bar and a ballroom. While there were also staff quarters available, the Perelson did not have anybody employed full-time, so seemingly this was an unused part of the home. With these many lavish features, it is clear this was not the average family home. The house is located in the affluent suburb of Los Feliz, Los Angeles, a quiet corner of a busy city. The house was bought for $60,000—approximately half a million dollars today (Maysh, 2019).

Neighbors remember the Perelson kids as happy, unassuming children who caused no trouble. Particularly, those who knew Judye described her as being sweet. Her 1958 yearbook from Barrister High School documents that she was a member of the Girls League and a secretary for the student body council. These were well-rounded all-American kids living everyday life.

Beginning of the end

By 1959, only a few years after the mansion's purchase, Harold Perelson found himself in immeasurable financial strife. The syringe he invented was losing him money. Despite it being his grand creation, it was not the commercial powerhouse he anticipated. He had entered into a contract with a man allegedly named Edward Shustack, who promised to turn the syringe into a marketable item. They planned to split the profits. It is reported that Harold and Lillian contributed $24,496 to this project, much of it from their savings. This seemed to be the beginning of the end for this family.

In 1952, Harold accused Shustack of using a fake name and willfully misleading him. The court proceedings lasted several years and burned through the remainder of the Perelsons' money. Reporter Jeff Maysh quotes a letter from Judye as saying, "My family is on the merry-go-round again, same problems, same worries, only tenfold ... My parents, so to speak, are in a bind financially." Judye wrote this right before the attacks took place.

This was not the only financial strain on the family. In 1957, Judye was driving her parents' car when she got into an accident, with both her siblings as passengers. "Judye suffered hand and knee injuries, concussion, and 'severe shock'. Young Joel had a head injury and 'severe shock to the nervous system'; and Deborah's cheek was sliced open" (Maysh, 2019). The medical bills for the children were costly. To assist with these payments, Harold took the other driver to court, seeking $50,000 to cover the expenses of the accident. He only won $10,000, barely enough to cover the children's medical bills, once again losing more on a court case than he won, since the legal fees exceeded the restitution. This was another financial blow he could not afford.

These issues effected mental strain on the patriarch of the family and his psychological health. He had a few heart attacks, which impacted his ability to work and even led to hospitalization.

This series of events defined the last few years of the Perelson family's lives. The financial stress Harold Perelson felt changed everything. Even for those who survived, life would never be the same.

Terrifying Awakening

For many across the world, December is a time spent with family. It is a merry season, with Christmas in full swing and the new year just around the corner. Unfortunately, this was not the case for the Perelson family in 1959. In the very early morning of December 6th, Harold Pereleson began a brutal attack on his family, which has remained in the public consciousness decades after it happened.

At 4:30 am, armed with a ball-peen hammer, Harold struck his wife in the back of her head. Lillian did not see the attack coming, and did not even have time to scream and warn her children. While his wife bled out onto their bed, Harold walked to his eldest daughter's room and lashed out at her with the same hammer. Judye was aware of the attack and raised her arm in defense, softening the impact. She survived the blow and screamed so loudly that a few close neighbors were alerted to the horrors taking place at the house.

Judye was disoriented and confused, but alert. Harold advised his daughter to "lay still" and "be quiet" (Maysh, 2019); luckily, she did not comply. She played dead until he left, then ran from her bedroom to her parents' room, looking for her mother. After seeing what her father had done, Judye ran to her neighbors, banging on all their doors until they came to help. Doctor Cheri Lewis, a former babysitter of the two younger Perelson children, remembers this early morning vividly. Judye entered their home, her body soaked in blood (Pool, 2009). The Lewis family was very close with the Perelsons, and they could not believe what they were seeing. From their home, Judye was rushed to Central Receiving Hospital, and then to General Hospital, where she was treated for a possible skull fracture and extreme bruising.

Her scream also woke her two younger siblings. The Los Angeles Times reported: "When the victim's screams awakened two younger children, Perelson told them they simply had a bad dream, his youngest daughter told police. 'Go back to bed. This is a nightmare,' he told 11-year-old Debbie. As a result, she and her thirteen-year-old brother, Joel, escaped injury" (Pool, 2009).

As this was happening, Marshall Ross, another family neighbor, entered the home after hearing the scream and commotion. He found the two younger children hiding on the first floor, uninjured. He continued upstairs to inspect what else had happened, where he came face to face with Harold. According to the coroner's report, Harold told Marshall to go home and not bother him before walking to the bathroom (Pool, 2009). Without knowing the horrors of what Harold had done, Marshall did not think to apprehend the doctor.

Upon entering the bathroom, Dr. Perelson rummaged through the medicine cabinet. In the process, he covered every surface he touched in the blood of his wife and daughter. He searched until he found the drug Nembutal, a fast-acting barbiturate. This is the drug that supposedly killed Judy Garland, and has been a common drug for attempting suicide. Harold took several other pills to ensure that he would not survive, including codeine and other powerful tranquilizers. He left little up to chance. His experience in the medical field-assisted with this, as he knew what had the highest chance of ending his life quickly. The doctor then went to bed and waited for the drugs to kill him.

The LAPD arrived fifteen minutes after Marshall Ross entered the house and found Harold Perelson in the bed, hammer still in hand and covered in blood. While he was still breathing at that time, he would be dead before the ambulance arrived. Lillian died in her bed from asphyxiation — after she was attacked, she drowned in her own blood.

This was how the horrendous events of that early morning ended. Both Harold and Lillian were dead, Judye was severely beaten, and all three children were orphans.

Investigation

Despite both formal and informal investigations into this case, it is still unclear why things seemed so dire that Harold saw this as his only option. Over the years, both detectives and amateur sleuths have pored over the details of the murders, looking for answers. Unfortunately, the surviving family members have disappeared into anonymity. Unlike many survivors of famous criminal cases, they have not spoken publicly about their ordeal, so the entire night remains shrouded in secrecy. Despite decades of people searching for any details that they can find about the Perelsons, there is still very little known about them. Due to the lack of information, anything remotely linked to the family has become fodder for speculation.

The police investigation into this case began almost immediately. One of the first notable findings was the book on Harold's nightstand—a copy of Dante's *The Divine Comedy,* opened to a page that reads "Midway upon the journey of our life I found myself within a forest dark, for the straightforward pathway had been lost" (Maysh, 2019). This passage is enough to spark several theories about what Harold thought as he planned and executed his attack on his family. An obvious interpretation is that this was a truly lost man who believed he had no choice but to murder his family to save them from the shame his financial issues would bring. This is not a straightforward path, though it would be one that ended his struggles for good. His actions remain inexcusable, no matter his mindset or inner battles, though insight into his mind is a fascinating part of understanding the horror of this story.

Police also searched the family cars, which is where they found the note from Judye to her aunt that spoke of the financial crisis her parents were facing. In this letter, it is reported that Judye also spoke of finding a job to help her parents during this time, as she found it difficult to watch them struggle. These two pieces of evidence created a clear-cut case for the police. The family's main breadwinner was in apparent financial distress, which was causing him medical issues, and he saw that ending the lives of those in his family would be the way to spare them from the troubles his mistakes had caused. Which unfortunately, resulted in two deaths and lives ruined.

Investigators found that the family had a seemingly ordinary night on December 5th. Based on witness statements from the children and evidence found at the crime scene, the family ate dinner together that night without incident and casually went to bed. The rest of the family was not privy to Harold's inner turmoil, so what happened in the time between saying goodnight to his family and 4:30 am, when he killed his wife?

For those close to the Perelsons, the police investigation wasn't enough. They needed more information, and sought to do their research. The Lewis family is a prime example of friends who could not deal with the tragedy without looking into it themselves. Cheryl Lewis recalls how highly strung her mother was during this time, as she and Harold were particularly close. Her father, a lawyer, decided to find any information he could on his former friend. He found the heart attacks that hospitalized the doctor and kept him from working were not heart attacks at all.

They were suicide attempts.

Suicide is not a marker of someone with murderous intentions, so this does not explain Harold's actions. Instead, it creates more questions. If he wanted to end his own life, why did he turn on his family in such a drastic way? The Lewis family speculates that perhaps he was going after the people he viewed as creating his problem, or that his wife may have looked to have him committed, and he could not stand the embarrassment this would bring (Maysh, 2019). Though it does not ease the pain of anyone affected, this is still the best motive found to explain why this horrendous act occurred.

The main inconsistency and reason for speculation in this case is why Harold attacked his family rather than only kill himself.

Also, why did he not attack his two younger children? Suppose we accept the theory that he wanted to protect his family from future embarrassment, financial hardship, and further struggles. Would he not then seek to murder his entire family? Did he find it too difficult to attack his smaller children, given they were more defenseless, or was there another reason why Judye was the only one he came after? Evidence suggests that Judye was the only one of the three children who knew about their father's financial issues, so perhaps Harold sought to murder those aware of his strife.

There is also evidence to suggest that Lillian's family knew about the deep financial troubles Harold was facing. It is not clear if they received this information from Lillian or Judye; however, there is documentation that shows her sister Gertrude Saylan "petitioned to take over as trustee for the children's compensation payments from the car accident" (Maysh, 2019). Without knowing that the family was in trouble, Gertrude would have been no reason to do this. Unfortunately, despite her best efforts, she was unable to save her sister from her horrific fate.

In the decades since the murder-suicide, study and discussion of mental health issues have advanced considerably. Modern-day psychologists have profiled Harold as a narcissist. Doctor Adams, a psychologist who specializes in the study of men who murder their families, states that "many of these guys, these types of perpetrators, are very invested in their public image;" and "when there is a prospect that their reputation or status can be harmed, they suffer a narcissistic injury. [Their murders] are almost like a type of damage control" (Maysh, 2019). As Harold left no suicide note, there is no way of confirming these assertions, though they are the closest thing to an answer.

As mentioned, the Perelson children went into hiding after the events of December 6th, 1959. Though it was initially thought that Harold's family took them in, it has since been found that it was Lillian's family. The children moved to the east coast, changed their names, and have not been publicly heard from since. Despite numerous attempts to find and interview them, they have not come forward to tell their story and have lived their lives in anonymity.

Paranormal Encounters

Like any story with a gruesome murder at the center, it is unsurprising that stories about paranormal sightings and encounters have followed. Despite nobody living in the home since the death of the Perelson family, numerous people have found themselves on the premises with various stories about what they saw.

Often, the people who visited the Los Feliz Mansion were squatters who knew it would be empty. For a long time, the property didn't have security cameras, so they would go undetected for as long as they wanted. Another group that would venture into the home were neighborhood kids looking to find out if the ghost stories they heard were true. No matter the motive of the visitor, the reports of what these trespassers witnessed are bone-chilling. While roaming the house, people reported hearing whispers, voices, and moans throughout the mansion. In an empty room, whispers would begin out of nowhere. The house itself had an eerie, unsettling feel. Even more terrifying, some have heard a woman screaming, followed by a thud and punctuated silence.

Similarly, some report the moans of a man in despair, followed by the same slow, horrible silence. A strange feeling permeates the house, making those inside fear that something terrible was about to happen. This apprehension lingers, then the screaming woman would be heard. Those who attempted to occupy the house soon found it was not a good place for shelter and would quickly leave. Often, they felt as though the dread of the house were following them.

The mansion was not a welcoming host to any guests.

People who have been brave enough to approach the house without going inside have shared similar stories of the mansion's eerie and distressing aura. They have claimed that just a short visit to see the house left them with feelings of dread and overwhelming despair. Those who have peaked through the windows have also claimed to see the face of a woman appear, then disappear just as quickly. There is no physical evidence of this, as the occurrence happens so fast nobody has been able to capture an image of it. It is theorized that perhaps the woman cannot be photographed.

The neighbors also tell fascinating stories about those who have lived at the mansion in the years since the attacks. Those who reside near the Los Feliz Mansion have had their fair share of spooky sightings and experiences over the years. One neighbor, Sheree Waterson, explored the house one night, curious about what she could find. Unfortunately for her, this was after burglar alarms had been installed. These went off as she entered through the back door of the property, but her adventure to the house was not without incident. As she opened the back door, a spider bit her and her hand began throbbing with pain. The bite was so severe that blood streaked her hand. She was treated by a doctor for this shortly after. Sheree claims that her own back door alarm would randomly be triggered and go off in the following days, though nobody was there. She said, "It was like the ghost was following us" (Maysh, 2019). Other neighbors have reported hearing the mansion's alarm system being triggered without cause. There would be nobody near the property, and yet, it would sound through the neighborhood.

In his book, *Hollywood Obscura,* author Brian Clane explores what paranormal investigators and ghost hunters have found at the mansion. These reports echo what squatters, visitors, and neighbors alike have said. The ghost hunters specifically focused on the spirit of a woman at the property, who seems to be terrified of something. She is known to yell "no" in distress, to scream, and then to disappear. An eerie silence then engulfs the house. They have also witnessed a woman who stares out of the upstairs windows, then vanishes before anybody can capture proof of her existence.

Without concrete evidence of paranormal activity, it is easy to dismiss the claims of ghosts and hauntings at the Los Feliz Mansion. With such a dark history, it is entirely possible that visitors and experts have heard the creaks of an old home and attributed them to ghosts, or have had overactive imaginations while on the property. While this is possible, it is also difficult to dismiss these claims, as they have come from so many sources, all of whom have experienced similar occurrences while at the house.

In paranormal circles, it is assumed that those who have experienced extreme violence or a shocking end to their life may be trapped at the place of their death. Another possibility is that the spirit died so unexpectedly that they did not realize they needed to cross over. So, did this happen to Lillian Perelson? Is the ghost of Harold Perelson also trapped with her? Though there is no way of knowing what is happening at the mansion for sure, it cannot be ignored that all those who have visited have left with an impending sense of dread and gloom. The troubled history of the home permeates through the walls and hallways, haunted or not.

The Los Feliz Mansion

The Los Feliz Mansion has stood mostly unoccupied since the Perelson family resided there. This has sparked an increased fascination in the home, as it stands to be a time capsule for a way of life from many decades ago. The obsession with the mansion is two-fold. First, there is the fixation on the murder-suicide and the horrors experienced by the Perelson family. With the rise of true-crime podcasts and television shows, the hype around the Los Feliz Mansion has only increased, with a legion of new enthusiasts in every generation. Second, that the home remains untouched has sparked even more interest in the property. A property is rarely left standing with no occupants in a busy city like Los Angeles, so this has only expanded the allure of this house.

Despite its lack of residence, the mansion was sold very shortly after the Perelson family lived there. Emily and Julian Enriquez purchased it in 1960, a mere year after the attacks, though they never moved into the house. Over the decades, the house fell into disrepair, though the neighbors have helped with the upkeep as much as they could. Many of them complained about the unwelcome visitors who unlawfully squatted at the property, so burglar alarms and security systems were installed in the 1990s. Unfortunately, this did not stop paranormal tourists from coming to the home, particularly as it was rumored to be left in the exact condition as the night of the murder. People would visit to peek through the windows of the house to catch a glimpse of the Christmas tree that still stood in the living room, and the rest of the untouched house. The excitement of knowing that you could see how the Perelsons lived was too enticing for many to ignore.

Unfortunately, it seems that the rumors that the house had not been touched since the Perelson family are likely untrue. In his investigative piece, Jeff Maysh writes about several historical inaccuracies that have led him to conclude that these are not all the Perelson family's belongings (2019). His research comes from the photos of true-crime enthusiast Jennifer Cray, who once broke into the house and photographed many of the things she found there, uploading them to her blog. Maysh looked closely at these photos to find the inconsistencies. He points out that Spaghetti-O's in the kitchen were not marketed until 1965, so they could not have belonged to the Perelsons. He also notes a magazine from May 9th, 1960, another object that found its way onto the property after the murders. Most interestingly, he observes that the Christmas tree in the living room may not have belonged to the Perelsons, either. They were a Jewish family, and they may not have even celebrated Christmas. Of course, Christmas has become more of a cultural holiday than a religious one, so this is not a smoking gun—families across America, regardless of religious background, engage in the holiday merriment. As a result, it is a little more difficult to dispute the evidence found in the photos.

All these findings lead Maysh and others to believe that another family lived on the property for a short period. It is believed they must have moved there shortly after the attacks, as the magazine found was dated only five months later. The presumption is that a family moved there, unaware of the home's history, then on the anniversary of the murder-suicide, left in such a rush that they didn't have time to pack the Christmas presents under the tree. Others have also used this theory to add to their speculation. The house could have been so haunted that the family could not stand to live there any longer, particularly around the time of the anniversary, when the spirits may have been in more distress. Regardless of what is true, that the home remains untouched from any point in that period is fascinating. A family's life was left almost completely undisturbed within those walls, making this a one-of-a-kind monument, preserving the past.

Once the original purchasers of the house passed away in 1994, their son, Rudy Enriquez, inherited ownership. While he lived only a short drive away from the mansion, he chose not to live there. Instead, he used the house as storage, and other than the security alarms and minor improvements to the home, he made little effort to repair the house or return it to its former glory. The home's mailbox was always full, with nobody checking it. The antique fixtures were stolen or broken off, but otherwise the mansion remained largely untouched.

Rudy Enriquez passed away in 2016 and, for the first time in over fifty years, the Los Feliz Mansion went on the market. Despite the California Civil Code, which states that "Realtors are legally obliged to tell buyers of a material defect like a violent death— but only if the death occurred within three years of the date an offer is made to purchase the home" (Maysh, 2015), there was no way that this property could hide its dark history. According to the New York Post, the house was on the market until 2020 and was sold to a company named Luxmanor Custom Home Builders, which has not made any moves to alter or resell the house at this stage (Paynter, 2021). There is no doubt that the story of the Los Feliz Mansion will not end here, and that eagle-eyed observers will continue to follow its story closely.

An Enduring Legacy

Something about the story of the Los Feliz Mansion has continued to interest people for almost sixty years. Whether it is the murders themselves or the legacy of the property, a mass of people still flock to the internet to read about, watch, and listen to the story of the Perelsons. Perhaps this is because there are so many unanswered questions that linger.

There will likely never be concrete answers to parts of this story. Harold Perelson's motive will never be fully clear. Over the years, with advances in mental health studies, it has become apparent that he was battling inner demons; however, certain parts of the attacks do not match up. For example, why did he attempt to murder one of his children, and not all? Why did he not just kill himself? Is there anything more to the story at all, or is this just the case of another broken man who took his family down with him? With so much unknown, it is impossible to imagine that the fascination with this case will not live on.

If you enjoyed this story, I'd love it if you could leave a review. I'd also like to hear from you! Have you experienced anything spooky? Do you believe in the supernatural?

CHAPTER 3:
THE STANLEY HOTEL

ID YOU KNOW THAT A REAL PLACE INSPIRED THE HOTEL IN *THE SHINING*? Did you know people are still visiting it to this day to find the many ghosts that reside there? Would you believe the tales that come from eyewitnesses who swear they saw the paranormal?

Welcome to the story of the Stanley Hotel.

The Stanley Hotel, in Estes Park, Colorado, is considered to be one of the most haunted hotels in the world. It has been referred to as a "Disneyland for ghosts" and is one of the most paranormal spots that people can still visit. With hundreds of guests seeing different spirits and supernatural occurrences on the property, it is difficult to dismiss the notion that this resort has something spooky happening on its premises.

Lord Dunraven originally purchased the land where the hotel was built in 1862, hoping to create a hunting ground. However, this was unpopular with the residents of the area. Lord Dunraven left the area, where nothing significant happened until 1909, when Freelan Oscar Stanley found his way to Colorado and saw this location as the perfect place to build a grand hotel.

The hotel itself is a beautiful sight to see. With a stunning grand staircase leading to each floor and state-of-the-art features, there is no denying that Stanley put everything he had into making this a place of luxury. The hotel boasts 140 rooms and offers a beautiful view of the Rocky Mountains. With a stunning white exterior and historical feel, it has since been refurbished to keep up with modern times. It now runs ghost tours, and fans of the supernatural tend to book the most haunted rooms.

There is no shortage of visitors who have come to the hotel purely to witness the unexplained. Even on their website, the hotel advertises its supernatural history and has strongly leaned into its reputation. However, like any paranormal story, there is no shortage of people who simply do not believe the tales told.

So, should we believe the hundreds of eyewitness accounts, or is this nothing more than rumors and speculation about the supernatural? No matter what side of the fence you choose to sit on, it is certainly clear that the Stanley Hotel is one of the most interesting haunted venues in America. Believer or not, join me as I tell you the tale of this fascinating resort.

The Stanley Hotel

In 1909, Freelan Oscar Stanley, the inventor of the Yankee steam-powered car, finished building his latest project — the Stanley Hotel. It was built about five miles from the entrance of the Rocky Mountains in Colorado, where Stanley had spent the last few years recovering from tuberculosis. His doctor advised that he needed fresh air, and there was no air fresher than what he found in the mountains. After recovering from his illness, he began building a resort that catered to the upper class. He and wife, Flora, fell in love with the area and weren't ready to leave it just yet.

The Stanley Hotel was created to be a summer resort, so it lacked heating but had all the other amenities its guests could possibly desire. It had running water and electricity, two things which were not yet taken for granted in this era. In addition to these, Stanley ensured visitors would experience all kinds of luxury while staying at his resort.

The hotel has a dazzling history featuring many famous and prestigious guests. These guests include President Theodore Roosevelt, composer John Philip Sousa, Titanic survivor "The Unsinkable Molly Brown," and the Emperor and Empress of Japan (Weiser, 2019). Scenes from the movie *Dumb and Dumber* were even filmed at the resort (Barber, 2014). Perhaps most notably, world-famous horror writer Stephen King visited the hotel, and later based one of his most famous novels on his stay at the property. *The Shining* tells the story of a struggling writer who takes his family along when he takes a job as a winter caretaker at a hotel in the Colorado Rockies. In reality, while staying at the Stanley Hotel, King and his wife were the only guests. The location, with its spooky history, greatly inspired him to write this novel (Beahm, 1995).

Despite its history as a hotel for the stars, there is also a dark underbelly to the Stanley Hotel. It is theorized that the resort was built on the remains of an ancient Native American burial ground, and therefore was cursed before it even opened its doors. There are even stories of Native American ghosts being seen on the premises (Arnett, 2018).

The Stanley Hotel has a reputation for being incredibly haunted. Over the span of decades, hundreds of people have seen the same recurring ghosts on the property. What is surprising for many to learn is that the hotel itself doesn't have a deadly history. Unlike other haunted venues, there has not been an abundance of death on the property. Rather, it seems ghosts are drawn to the location for some other reason. Paranormal investigator, Richard Estep, believes "we're seeing people coming back because they deeply love this hotel" (Earls, 2019).

This begs the questions: What ghosts are haunting the halls and rooms of the Stanley Hotel? Where did they come from? And how did they end up there?

Hauntings and Encounters

The Stanley Hotel is a hotspot for paranormal activity. Many psychics and believers have named it as one of the top ten most haunted places in America (Arnett, 2018). Nowadays, hundreds of visitors go to the hotel in hopes of spotting one of the many ghosts that have been sighted on the grounds over the years.

Overall, researchers and witnesses claim that most of the spirits haunting the Stanley Hotel are not vengeful. Rather, they actually seem friendly. There are few stories of scary hauntings or people being hurt by the ghosts. At most, people are surprised and pleased to see the mystical apparitions that appear before them.

Many different ghosts appear at the hotel. There is no way to know precisely how many spirits reside at the estate, but there are several that appear repeatedly, to be seen by many visitors. Some guests have even managed to snap photographs of these supernatural entities. There is no clear consensus about whether these ghosts know they are alive or dead. Some still interact with guests, while others seem to be spooked by the cleaning staff. Who knew ghosts were scared of vacuum cleaners?

The Concert Hall

It is no surprise that visitors often spot the ghosts of Freelan and Flora around the Stanley Hotel. The couple loved their home dearly and undoubtedly wanted to settle there as they passed into the eternity of the supernatural. Many guests have spotted Flora in the Concert Hall. Sometimes, the sounds of the piano ring through the hall even though nobody is playing. Many believe this is actually Flora at the keys, making music. In life, she was a talented musician and spent much of her time entertaining her guests. Some assume she still plays to keep up with the tradition. Though the Stanley Hotel isn't quite as grand as it once was, it seems the ghost of Flora won't let it be without music. Stanley gifted the Concert Hall to Flora, and it seems to be where she has found her final resting place.

Another ghost which is seen in the Concert Hall has been named Paul. The spirit of Paul is often heard enforcing a curfew to guests. Many have heard him telling them to "get out," and most reports say this comes after 11:30 p.m. One construction worker also had a run-in with Paul. The man felt that something was nudging him repeatedly while he was sanding the floors of the hall. He eventually left because the feeling wouldn't stop. Paul also seems to enjoy having a bit of fun with tour groups that come to see the haunted hall. He is said to be responsible for flickering lights that give visitors a bit of a scare. Sometimes, he'll even flash the lights upon request! Though Paul has hurt no one, it seems he likes to be a bit of a nuisance. Some theorize that the ghost is someone who used to work at the hotel and found happiness there. Perhaps after death, they decided to come back to live among the many other spirits in the resort. Either way, Paul is a popular ghost and is often sought out by those coming to get a glimpse of the supernatural.

The Concert Hall is also home to a ghost named Lucy, described as a young girl who often is spotted in the hall and the basement.

There is no confirmed story of who Lucy was when she was alive, though some believe that she was potentially a runaway or a homeless person who found a home at the hotel for a brief period of time (Anas, 2020). An alternative, more sinister theory, is that she was a young girl who snuck into the hotel and was caught spying on the construction plans. According to this story, when hotel workers found her, they threw her out into the cold to freeze to death (O'Neill, 2019). There is no confirmation of her death, but Lucy has been favorable to paranormal investigators and presents herself to them through flashing lights. She seems to have confirmed some aspects of this theory. One tour group even captured a photo of her. She was photographed wearing a hot pink dress. When the person who took the picture showed it to everyone, they confirmed they had not seen this girl on the tour with them, nor had anyone matching her appearance been at the hotel that day. They came to the conclusion that this must have been Lucy. Others have had similar experiences with a girl in the same, or similar, outfit.

Room 217

Fans of Stephen King might know this room number as Room 237. However, the spookiest room in the Stanley Hotel, and the room King stayed in, is room 217. This is just one aspect of The Stanley Hotel that inspired *The Shining*. However, the hauntings that happen in this room differ greatly from what the novelist eventually wrote about.

In the early days of the hotel's existence, there was a gas leak that almost killed one of its staff. The head housekeeper at the time,

Elizabeth Wilson, was lighting the gas lamps in the room when it exploded. She was blasted through the floor and into the dining room below. Fortunately, Mrs. Wilson survived, and after she recovered from her injuries, came back to work at the hotel. She remained until she was ninety years old and was one of the most loyal staff members the hotel has ever seen. One theory is that after spending her entire adult life working and caring for this hotel, it only made sense that she would return there to make it her final resting place. Elizabeth Wilson has made her presence known to many guests, and people have said that "Mrs. Wilson does what she wants, to who she wants" (Earls, 2019).

Elizabeth Wilson has been known to have issues with unmarried couples who stay in room 217. Many have reported that they felt as though there was an invisible wedge between them during the night, preventing them from reaching one another. They have described it as otherworldly, and couldn't quite put their finger on where the eerie feeling came from. Some even described it as a cold force separating them. Likewise, single men have woken up and found all their belongings to be packed up and moved outside of the room, ready for them to leave. She has also continued some of her housekeeping duties. In some instances, guests have woken up to find their clothes folded, shoes put away, and the room generally tidied. Even though she doesn't take to unmarried couples and single men, Elizabeth is seemingly a helpful spirit who just wants the place to be nice and clean, like it was in her day.

The Fourth Floor

On the fourth floor of the Stanley Hotel, there is an abundance of ghostly activity. To start, there are reports of a cowboy roaming room 428. Researchers believe this to be the spirit of Jim Nugent, also known as "Rocky Mountain Jim," who died in 1874. He was famously opposed to the plans of the original landowner, Lord Dunraven, to turn the ranch into a hunting ground. Jim eventually passed away nearby. Some believe his ghost took up residence at the hotel from the moment it was built. People who have encountered Jim have said he is a friendly cowboy who sometimes gives a ghostly kiss to the lady visitors of that room. Some women have claimed to feel the presence of something kissing their foreheads at night, though he has always been respectful to those he has encountered. One couple even politely asked him to leave, and he obliged (O'Neill, 2019). Some have reported seeing a cowboy sitting at the edge of their bed. Even though he is a gentleman, it is still understandably a very spooky thing to occur while staying at a hotel.

This room has also seen other paranormal activity. However, some of these experiences could not be tied to the cowboy. Some guests reported hearing furniture being moved throughout the night when there was nobody else in the room, while others said they heard the sounds of footsteps coming from the floor above throughout the night. Tour guides note, however, that it is impossible to hear footsteps above that room because it is on the top floor of the hotel, leading many to assume this is yet another ghostly happening.

Most of the fourth floor used to be a cavernous attic before it was converted into rooms for guests. Prior to the renovation, the space would house female employees, their children, and some nannies who stayed on the property. This may explain why the sounds of kids laughing and playing are often heard from this area, particularly in room 401. People have spotted the ghosts of children in room 418, and some have witnessed things moving of their own accord. Others have had the sheets ripped from them during the night, and one child even claimed that a little boy was tickling her at night until she told him to stop. Children staying in room 418 have said that little boys and girls have asked them to play games. Some speculate that this is where Stephen King got the idea of the twins haunting the hotel in *The Shining*. Though there are no reports of any children dying on the property, many believe there are too many stories of children being heard and seen for it to be a coincidence. Perhaps they, too, have fond memories of being at the hotel.

Room 407 reportedly has a friendly ghost that tucks children into bed at night. One child claimed that when he kicked off his covers at night, a spirit came and put them back on him before disappearing. Other reports say the ghost in this room is none other than Lord Dunraven. He has been seen standing in the corner of the room, simply observing the guests with no malice or ill-intent. People have said that, similar to the cowboy, he is a fan of women and often shows his affection to them. He has been known to wrap his arm around women and play with their hair. Lord Dunraven has shown a slight dislike of men; some have said they felt a general unease when staying in this room, and sometimes reported missing belongings. Guests have also reported that the light in the room often turns off and on by itself, and that when it is on, one can see the outline of a man near the switch. Some have seen a supernatural figure appearing at the window of room 407, and his description matches that of the former landowner. The hotel staff have confirmed that people have noticed a man in the window even when the room unoccupied, and they have no logical explanation as to who that man could be.

There has also been a man spotted in room 413, yet another place on the fourth floor with ghostly activity. This man is unidentified, though he is described as wearing old-fashioned clothes that don't match the attire of the day. "Other reports have been made of a man's face in a blue ball resting outside of this room" (O'Neill, 2019). This was, of course, slightly frightening for guests, but not menacing or threatening to anyone.

Overall, it seems the fourth floor is a popular spot for ghosts to congregate. If you ever go to the Stanley Hotel and want to see the paranormal, make sure you book one of these rooms!

The Vortex Theory

The Vortex Theory refers to one of the most breathtaking parts of the Stanley Hotel: The staircase between floors which starts in the resort's lobby. There have been many strange occurrences that have intrigued (and sometimes scared) visitors. Many people have experienced random cold patches in this exact spot. Suddenly, it's as though they have walked through a frigid room. Then, it goes away like it never happened. Nothing explains this phenomenon, and it has led believers to think this has something to do with the supernatural. Perhaps even stranger, some guests have suddenly become dizzy when on the staircase, and have described the sensation of someone walking through them.

There have been paranormal investigators who have captured strange photos and videos in this section of the hotel, which they believe is proof of the supernatural beings that roam the area. They have photographic evidence of random orbs appearing, as well as unexplained distortions. Notably, the ghost of the owner, Freelan Oscar Stanley, has often been spotted here with his wife, Flora. He is usually seen at the Billiards Room and the bar, but many have also seen him here. It is almost as if he is still greeting his guests at one of the most important points of the place he loved so much.

The Vortex Theory surmises the grand staircase to be how ghosts travel from one world to another, like a portal between two worlds. The frequency of spiritual activity in this area inspires this theory, along with the fact that guest have spotted many different ghosts on the staircase. Instead of just one or two, it appears they have all passed through this section of the hotel at one time or another.

The Ghost of Billy

The icehouse was a room built in the original days of the hotel for the purpose of refrigeration. Since then, it has been converted into a museum and holds some of the original relics from the resort. Curiously, the ghost of a child has been spotted here a few times by visitors, and has even been photographed. This is the ghost of a young boy witnesses have named Billy.

Billy is said to have been seen throughout the hotel, and is very interactive with guests. He seems particularly in tune with people who have autism and developmental disorders (Hicks, 2019). He often plays with visitors' hair and shows himself to those he trusts. Staff have also noticed him a few times. Perhaps Billy is comfortable with people with autism because he experienced this in his lifetime or knew someone who did. He is an important figure in the hotel, and is near and dear to the hearts of those who have frequented the resort.

The Pet Cemetery

Another aspect of the hotel that Stephen King fans might recognize is the pet cemetery located on the property. The cemetery was made for the staff who lost their beloved pets and wanted them to be properly buried.

There have been sightings in the area of the spirits of two pets. One is a golden retriever named Cassie, and the other is the ghost of a fluffy white cat named Comanche. Both can be heard around the property.

Is This Really Happening?

If you are a believer, it is understandable why so many have visited the Stanley Hotel. There is evidence of the supernatural in many photos that guests have taken, and the happenings on the property fascinate paranormal researchers.

If you are a skeptic, it can certainly be hard to believe that any of these stories are real. There is something to be said about the power of suggestion. It's entirely possible that people have heard tales of spirits before arriving at the hotel, and have either imagined the noises of the old resort to be ghosts or have outright fabricated a narrative to suit the hotel's paranormal history.

It is easy to explore all the examples of the supernatural, but what do the non-believers have to say?

Debunking and Skeptics

There is no supernatural location in the world that hasn't led to skeptics and non-believers attempting to debunk the stories told by eyewitnesses who are absolutely sure they have experienced something outside of this realm. One should not ignore this perspective, because the search for truth should involve considering all possibilities. It is difficult to know what is real and what is not, so listening to both sides of the story is important.

Just a Coincidence?

Could it be possible that everything happening at the Stanley Hotel is purely a coincidence? Supernatural debunkers certainly believe so. Skeptics who have visited the hotel for their own research have found the strange happenings are explainable by logic. For example, a window closing on its own isn't a sign of a ghost. Instead, it can simply be the wind blowing it closed.

Many say that if you enter a situation looking for signs of the supernatural, you will find them. For example, rather than attributing strange noises such as creaks and groans to be the naturally occurring sounds of an aging property, one might assume these sounds are being caused by ghosts.

Some have also attempted to debunk the photos taken at the property as fabrications or tricks of light. One example is a photo of a young girl standing at a window of the hotel. The person who took the photo says that when they snapped the shot, there was nobody present. But upon viewing the image, there was the unexplained presence of someone looking down at them. "I took the picture, so to see it blows my mind," the photographer in question said. (Keith, 2021). Those who do not believe that this is a genuine claim chalk it up to the curtain being tangled up in a certain way. Others believe it could be a mannequin that the photographer simply didn't notice.

Either way, there is no way of knowing what really happened.

Haunted Hotel?

Whether you are a skeptic, a believer, or just here for an interesting story, there is no denying that a visit to the Stanley Hotel would be a fascinating trip. There is so much rumored ghostly activity that one would be hard-pressed *not* to experience something out of the ordinary (even if you believe that it is only a coincidence).

It is rare for a property to be full of friendly ghosts, which makes this resort one of the most unique locations in the world. Filled with some truly interesting characters, it wouldn't hurt to bump into one or two.

However, none have found an answer as to why ghosts seem to congregate at this hotel specifically. Perhaps it has a strong vortex energy, or perhaps it is a safe space for spirits to reside. Maybe there is even something to the theory that the hotel was built on an ancient Native American burial ground.

CHAPTER 4:
THE GREY GHOST

T HE HISTORY OF THE GREY GHOST IS UNUSUAL, as it is the story of a haunting on a ship rather than at a home or institution. This story takes place on the *Queen Mary*, a bigger, faster, and more technologically advanced ship than the Titanic. Operating first as a luxury travel ocean liner, the *Queen Mary* experienced quite a transformation in its operational years, assisting the British army in World War II and creating quite a track record as one of the most famous ships in history.

During the war, the ship gained its nickname, the Grey Ghost, as it was painted a dull, gray color and could avoid torpedo attacks like a ghost moving in the night. Along with its conventional fame, the ship is also acknowledged as one of the most haunted locations in the world. Now docked in Long Beach, California, the *Queen Mary* is visited by those interested in its history and paranormal tales. Many hope they will see one of the many ghosts that are said to roam the decommissioned vessel.

The History of the Grey Ghost

The construction of the *Queen Mary* was completed in 1935, and it made its maiden voyage that following year after being inspected by King Edward VIII. It quickly became the luxury ocean liner of choice, with royals and other dignitaries alike praising its speed and safety. In these first few years, the ship achieved many accolades, becoming one of the fastest and most powerful ships built in history. However, this wasn't the only impressive thing about the *Queen Mary*. The ship was enormous and boasted luxurious amenities for its impressive lineup of passengers. It had five dining areas, a remarkable ballroom, two pools, and a few beauty salons.

Along with this, first-class passengers had a special menu for their voyage featuring only the best food available. Celebrities like Clark Gable and politicians like Winston Churchill were some of the most famous travelers; however, the British Royal Family would undoubtedly be the most impressive of the ship's passengers. Notably, this included Queen Elizabeth II.

For those who could not afford first-class, there was the option to travel in second- or third-class, which was an entirely different experience from the wealthy. These people would sleep in overcrowded rooms near the crew and would not have access to any of the deluxe amenities their fellow passengers enjoyed. Nonetheless, it was exciting to be part of the history of the *Queen*

Mary. This was an opportunity like no other, and those who scored a ticket were in awe of the experience.

After just a few years of transporting the wealthy, the *Queen Mary* was repurposed to assist wartime efforts. In 1939, when England and France declared war on Germany, crew members began to black out the ship's portholes and sent her to New York. Along with her sister ship, the *Queen Elizabeth,* she was now a wartime vessel. The ship was painted a dark battleship gray, and all external remnants of what was once an extravagant vessel were gone. The ship transported troops from New York to Sydney and Singapore; it carried 10,000 soldiers and crew, and was an instrumental part of the Allied powers' logistics. The second reason for the nickname came from the incredible speed the Grey Ghost exhibited, seemingly having the ability to outrun any torpedo aimed at it. The ship was so fast that Adolf Hitler put out a bounty to sink it.

In October 1942, the Grey Ghost encountered its first real trouble when it collided with the light cruiser Curacoa, which was also from Britain. This horrendous accident claimed nearly four hundred lives, with soldiers dying either from impact or hypothermia as they were thrown into freezing waters. Survivors aboard the Curacoa recalled watching the *Queen Mary* coming towards them and knowing it would crash into them. The Naval Historical Society of Australia quotes the experience of one surviving seamen who watched the events unfold: "The gap narrowed inexorably as the stunned Watson finally found his vocal cords and screamed, 'She's going to ram us.'". Later, Watson described how many of his mates had been so shocked they could not move.

By the end of the war, it is estimated that the *Queen Mary* transported 800,000 service people and was a valuable contributor to the war's success (Naval Historical Society of Australia, 1998). In addition, at the end of the war, the Grey Ghost transported wartime babies and wives to the United States and Canada. These were called the bride and baby voyages, and the ship completed thirteen of these.

With its wartime service completed, the Grey Ghost made its final military voyage in 1946 from Halifax, Canada, back to England. After it was restored to its former glory, the ship began operating as a cruise liner again, attracting famous and wealthy passengers just like before. In 1951, Walt Disney took the *Queen Mary* to attend the European opening of his film *Alice In Wonderland*. Winston Churchill once again traveled on the ship, on one occasion to meet with President Harry S Truman and then again to meet with President Dwight D Eisenhower. Even Queen Elizabeth II returned for another trip on the majestic liner. These were viewed as the *Queen Mary*'s golden years.

In the 1960s, the *Queen Mary* saw a decline. Air travel was becoming far more prominent, and those who could afford to travel in the first-class cabins of the ship were favoring airplanes, as they were faster. The ship was no longer a modern vessel, and with the world turning its attention elsewhere, the decision was made to decommission the cruise liner altogether. Since 1967, the ship has been docked at Long Beach in California. It is now a popular tourist destination, with different sections of the ship restored to recreate various parts of the *Queen Mary*'s history. Tours run throughout the ship, and events are often held there.

The ship also contains a hotel where visitors can stay on board. Even though it is no longer functioning as a seabound vessel, the *Queen Mary* remains an integral part of modern-day history.

Hauntings Aboard the *Queen Mary*

The paranormal activity on the ship is so prevalent that Time Magazine labeled the *Queen Mary* as one of the "top 10 most haunted places on Earth" (Dobson, 2018). Throughout its existence, the *Queen Mary* recorded almost fifty deaths on board, not to mention the mass casualties recorded when the ship collided with the Curacoa. With this many unfortunate events happening on the ship, it is completely unsurprising that the Grey Ghost has a supernatural history like no other. It is estimated that roughly 150 spirits are onboard the *Queen Mary* today.

There are a few key characters that guests have witnessed over the years who have made themselves most known. For example, there is the ghost of a woman in an all-white evening gown who dances by herself throughout the luxury suites, which used to be called the Queen's Salon. She has been aptly dubbed the Woman in White or the White Lady, and is thought to be a first-class passenger who died aboard the ship (Dobson, 2018). The history of this woman is a mystery, however, she is often sighted by visitors and staff alike. Her spirit seems to float as she dances, and some tourists have even attempted to snap photographs of her. Unlike other ghosts, she does not disappear in the presence of a camera, and some believe they have proof of her existence on film. This woman's energy is very pleasant, and guests have typically had positive experiences when witnessing her. Despite how spooky it is to see a ghost, those who have spotted the White Lady have spoken positively of her. She is seemingly just a spirit who likes to dance through the halls to unheard music, and does not recognize that there are people around her. As far as ghost sightings go, this is one of the most positive interactions a person could have. There are also reports of another lady in white who has been spotted near the lobby, who is seen less often and is likely not the same ghost as the dancing lady.

One spirit whose death is accounted for in historical documentation is that of John Peddler. John was an eighteen-year-old crew member who died a very unfortunate end on the *Queen Mary* in 1966. The weight of a heavy door that trapped him crushed or severed him in half. He was reportedly playing chicken with another crew member when he became trapped and unable to escape the watertight door, though this is not verified, as the reason he was in this door is still unknown. Another theory is that he was trapped during a routine drill and could not be rescued. The site of his death, door thirteen in the shaft alley, is one of the most popular places to visit on the ship. Often, people claim to see John, and he has also been known to leave handprints behind on surfaces in this area. Some say that he is why screaming can be heard in that part of the ship, as his death was gruesome. When John is spotted, he is wearing blue overalls. Over time, the ghost of John has been nicknamed Half Hatch Harry and has been transformed into somewhat of a supernatural monster, though no sightings of him claim that he is anything more than a spirit in distress. In fact, in 2019, a petition was started requesting the official *Queen Mary*

Halloween event stop depicting John as a monster, as he was a real man who had a family left behind after his tragic accident. Despite this portrayal of him as something scary or horrific, his ghost remains one of the most sought after on the ship.

There is another young man who died aboard the ship named John Henry, who worked in the boiler room of the *Queen Mary*, and whose death is similar to that of John Peddler. At just seventeen, John Henry lied about his age to work on the ship during the war, and unfortunately died a horrible death. When a fire broke out on this part of the ship, he could not escape and was crushed to death while trying to flee. He died in engine room thirteen, which is now another one of the most popular spots to visit. Those who have been there claim to have heard knocking and screaming attributed to him, and have also seen unexplained smoke. Certain parts of this room randomly become hot to the touch, particularly the engine room door. It will also get very hot in the room, then go very cold. Current *Queen Mary* staff often hear unexplained banging and violent noises in the boiler room, which they believe is the ghost of John Henry.

One of the most horrible stories from the *Queen Mary* ghosts is Dana, who was reportedly shot dead in her room. Her family, including her mother and sisters, were strangled. The killer and motive for these killings are still unknown. Their room, B-474, is said to be one of the most haunted spots on the ship, and many have been scared to visit it due to its dark history. Despite this, the ghost of Dana has shown no ill-intent to visitors. She can sometimes be heard calling for her mother, or found playing. Dana is also known to wander other parts of the cabin and is sometimes seen in the swimming pool area and the boiler room.

Another well-known sighting is the ghost of a man dubbed the Tall Man. This is the figure of a dark, tall man who is dressed in a 1930s suit. He is often spotted in the first-class suites, and appears just as quickly as he disappears. He always seems to be happy; guests and staff say he smiles at them as he passes, and he has even been known to strike up a conversation with a visitor or two. His presence has supposedly been the cause of phones ringing in rooms with nobody on the other line, and faucets turning on as people enter bathrooms.

In the captain's quarters, the ghost of Captain John Treasure Jones is sometimes spotted. John Treasure Jones captained the ship from 1965 to 1967, sailing it for its last voyage from England to Long Beach, California. Sadly, the captain passed away in 1993, and some have claimed that his spirit returned to the *Queen Mary*. Though there are no definitive sightings of him, people have claimed to smell cigar smoke in his former quarters. Those who worked with him have reported that this was a very common occurrence when he was on the ship. This is more difficult to understand, as John Treasure Jones did not die on the ship nor experience any known horrific event, though it is not unheard of that a ghost will return to a place it once worked or lived.

While these ghosts are thought to be quite friendly, some more sinister spirits haunt the *Queen Mary*. For example, there is the rumored spirit of a man who may be found in the lobby wearing a fedora who has yellowing, rotting teeth. Those who have encountered him have felt very dark energy in his presence. There is also the myth of a cook burned alive by his fellow crewmen, and his screams can be heard in the kitchens; this is another spirit that gives off a very uneasy feeling.

The Swimming Pool

While many parts of the *Queen Mary* have proved to have high ghost activity, nothing quite compares to what some have witnessed at the ship's two swimming pools. Several ghosts have been sighted in these areas.

First, there is the famous story of a young girl who drowned in the second-class swimming pool. She is called Jackie, or Little Jackie, and is known to wander this area, which has since been converted into a theater. Some say Jackie calls for her parents, and sometimes the sound of splashing water echoes around this part of the *Queen Mary*. Jackie is often spotted in the first-class swimming pool area as well, and she is frequently seen holding a teddy bear. In addition, there have been times when a little girl's voice can be heard singing children's lullabies to herself, which is also believed to be Jackie. Paranormal tourists and investigators have tested this by singing the songs themselves to see if anybody joins in, and some claim that this is sometimes enough to draw her out.

There is also the ghost of a young woman named Sarah. The stories surrounding the death of Sarah vary. Some psychics who have visited the ship believe Sarah was a young girl who drowned in the first-class pool, while others believe she is the spirit of a woman who was attacked and murdered in the pool's changing rooms. These are likely two separate spirits who share a name. Those who believe Sarah is a little girl like Jackie have often found the two playing together, and it appears they are good friends. Sarah seems to protect Jackie and is a little more playful and likely to interact with visitors. She has been known to slap guests, tug at their clothes, and even push them. Those who have seen the young woman called Sarah have had a darker experience. As Sarah was murdered, they have felt an uneasy air in the change rooms and have sometimes seen damp footsteps appear, leading from the rooms back to the pool and the pool deck. It would be impossible for wet footsteps to occur naturally in these areas, as the change rooms have not been in operation for decades.

Another famous ghost is often found at the first-class swimming pool. His name is Grumpy, and he has been known to growl at visitors who pass by him. He is usually seen at the swimming pool entrance, and people have reported smelling cigarettes as they walk past this area, which is often attributed to him. Some guests have even recorded audio of his grumblings. Sometimes, Grumpy can also be seen or heard near the boiler rooms, along with Dana and John Henry. It is unknown who Grumpy was in the living world, though he has made quite the impact on the visitors who come to see him in the spirit world.

Speaking more generally, the first-class swimming pool seems to be the epicenter of ghost activity. Visitors have claimed to see or hear all kinds of ghosts; ladies in 1930s style bathing suits lounging on the pool deck or children playing in the water, with the sound of splashing and giggling reverberating through the room. All these ghosts seem unbothered by the guests and in good spirits. Often, they don't seem to notice that there is anybody else there.

Other areas of the ship, which have also exhibited a high level of spirit activity, include the *Queen Mary* isolation ward, where any unwell passengers would go to prevent widespread illness. As this is where sick people were confined, many deaths occurred in this section of the ship. Those who have visited have claimed that this area has a very cold and heavy energy. Often, visitors are filled with dread for no reason. There are many voices heard in this area and sometimes screams of those in pain. While highly visited, this is an uneasy section of the ship.

The Vortex Theory

It is impossible to talk about the supernatural elements of the *Queen Mary* without looking at one of the most unique components of this story. While the ship is believed to be highly haunted, there is also a theory that the ship contains a vortex, or a gateway to another plane or another time. This supposed vortex is found in the ship's boiler room, which has proven to be a hotbed for ghost activity.

This is said to be how the ghosts travel from their time to the modern-day, and why many ghosts don't even realize that they are dead. It could also be a contributor to the sheer number of spirits that are on the *Queen Mary*. Visitors previously claimed to have experienced vortex-like energy on this part of the ship.

Some have also said that a vortex can be found in the women's changing room of the first-class swimming pool. This would explain the wet footprints found on the floor and would also be a good reason why so many ghosts are spotted in the pool area.

A particular ghost, a little boy named Daniel, is also part of the vortex theory. Some have seen Daniel come and go between planes, while others have had Daniel stop and stare at them, as though he is aware that they are there, but is unsure of who they are. Those who have spotted Daniel advise he is wearing a blue outfit and moves quickly.

While this may be too far-fetched for even those who believe in ghosts, it is an intriguing and unique element to the story of the Grey Ghost.

Staying Aboard the *Queen Mary*

Nowadays, it is possible to book a room and stay aboard the *Queen Mary*. Functioning as a hotel for visitors, the once lavish cruise liner-turned-warship takes on guests keen to experience both history and hauntings. Unlike many other famously haunted locations, the *Queen Mary* staff embraces this aspect of its history and accommodates those seeking a paranormal experience. This includes the opportunity to tour the ship with paranormal experts, who lead visitors through the most haunted spots searching for the ghosts who reside there. In addition, they run both day and night tours, hoping to assist visitors with finding a paranormal experience.

As mentioned previously, the *Queen Mary* also operates as a hotel. While this was not necessarily part of the paranormal experience, it does not stop guests from having ghostly encounters while staying the night. One such section of the ship was so haunted, and frightened guests so often, that it had to be closed for decades. This section of the vessel is called the B-deck and is located where the third-class cabins were. The once-cramped quarters have since been refurbished, and what was previously three rooms is now one large area created for the comfort of modern-day visitors. When these rooms first opened to the public, those who stayed were so horrified that they would leave in the middle of the night, demanding a refund for their stay. They might wake in the middle of the night to find a man standing over them, the phone would ring randomly with nobody on the other line, taps would turn on and off, and their blankets would be tossed clean off their bodies while they slept. Sometimes, guests would even emerge with scratches. The attacks were mostly centralized to room 340, and after numerous incidents occurred, the section closed.

Over time, however, the demand for this room and this section to reopen became too great for the current *Queen Mary* staff to ignore. People fascinated with the paranormal wanted the opportunity to experience such palpable supernatural energy, and many paranormal investigators were desperate to visit and see what they could find. Now, the ship's staff caters to such visitors, providing a ghostly package "including a chest with Ouija board for private seances, tarot cards, a crystal ball, and even ghost hunting equipment" (Dobson, 2018).

Does this acceptance of the paranormal by those who work at the *Queen Mary* invite skepticism? It has been theorized that the staff may be playing up the supernatural elements of the Grey Ghost, playing sounds throughout to make it seem like ghosts are making noises, planting foot and handprints as fake evidence, and even hiring actors to masquerade as ghosts. While this may be true, it could be true that ghosts roam the decommissioned ship, and those who have witnessed spirits and heard unexplained sounds had a paranormal experience.

CHAPTER 5:
PENITENTIARY OF HORRORS

G OTHIC BRICK PILLARS AND GUARD TOWERS LINE THE WALLS OF the Eastern State Penitentiary. Before being decommissioned in 1971, it housed many of America's most dangerous and well-known criminals. Now a museum and a Halloween attraction, one could almost forget about the horrors that took place inside. Still, the crumbled remains of inmates' cells and multiple accounts of unexplained phenomena keep the memory alive long after its closure.

Believers of the paranormal and reporters love to flock to this prison searching for ghosts, but the Eastern State Penitentiary was more than just a place where people lost their lives. People were tortured, driven to insanity, and murdered in this prison. Instead of being an institution where inmates were encouraged to repent and reform, it was a place where various torture methods instilled fear into their hearts. Many feel something unnatural is lurking within, but none could ever pinpoint the truth of it. Something is haunting this prison, but what could it be?

Penitent

Opening its doors in 1827, the Eastern State Penitentiary focused on a primary goal: to dismantle and reconstruct the treatment prison inmates faced. According to Dr. Benjamin Rush from The Philadelphia Society for Alleviating the Miseries of Public Prisons, inmates should regret their crimes and want to better themselves. To foster this environment, he argued a *penitentiary* must be created, rather than merely a prison.

Eight cellblocks branched out from a single guard tower in the middle of the facility. These cellblocks housed up to 250 inmates, and there was never a time when they were not full to bursting. This expensive, massive structure later became the blueprint for prisons around the world. More cellblocks were added, but the structural design resembling a wagon wheel from the initial blueprint stayed the same.

It was difficult to build on such a massive plot of land without running into financial hurdles. Upon completion, the penitentiary was considered one of America's most expensive buildings, and held that distinction for quite some time.

Eastern State Penitentiary was intended to make criminals feel remorse for committing their crimes, resulting in them turning to God to repent for their sins. It was a stark difference from the already established prisons, where most inmates were in the same cell, regardless of their background or crime. If there were punishments to administer, they were dealt with in the most gruesome fashion. Their inmates were no strangers to abuse and were subjected to multiple instances of whipping and branding.

The new penitentiary was supposed to be different, abandoning the tactic of unnecessary punishments for meaningful ones. Inmates were meant to be reformed, not face unspeakable torture. So, what went wrong?

Hell on Earth

When sentenced to the penitentiary, one was expected to realize the error of their ways someday. To achieve such an outcome, the belief was that the facility must instill guilt in the inmates. They had to be forced to recognize that what they did was wrong.

Each cell was furnished with a metal rack for a bed, a table, a toilet, and a Bible. These minimal furnishings were necessary to give the inmate the slightest comfort possible, aiming to make them turn to the Bible for guidance.

Inmates' cells had access to minimal sunlight, adding to the fear of their confinement. On the ceiling was a small skylight known as The Eye of God. With only this tiny sliver of light throughout the day, inmates were expected to look up at it and be reminded of God's embrace.

A host of torturous methods were used to correct the prisoners' behavior and force them to look for said guidance. Each punishment differed in severity, but they all intended to teach the inmates a lesson they would never forget.

Solitary Confinement

The primary method of making inmates repent was through solitary confinement. By keeping prisoners isolated from each other and the outside world, they were meant to turn to God to confess their sins.

Each prisoner was kept in their cell for almost the entire day, with their only outside contact lasting for one hour. To keep the inmates from learning the prison's layout, guards would place a thick hood over their heads so they could not see. Eyeholes were only added to the hoods after the early 1900s.

Prisoners were forbidden from speaking to one another or simply being in each others' presence. Even after the main restrictions on solitary confinement were lifted in 1913, they couldn't communicate with one another. They could be in the same vicinity when getting their food for the day, but they were forbidden from speaking. At night, the solitary confinement rules were the same as before.

Not only were prisoners not allowed to talk to other prisoners, but they also could not interact with the guards. When inmates were given their meals for the day, the guards handed them food through a small compartment in their door. To avoid letting the inmates know when the guards were coming, they would slip cloth over their shoes to mask their footsteps.

Instead of the inmates turning to God for repentance, the lack of human contact was enough to make the strongest person lose their sanity. Inmates would become so desperate for interaction, they would attempt to converse with one another while in their cells. Their primary methods of contact were through tapping the pipes or whispering through the vents. However, if they were caught—and they usually were—their punishment for breaking solitary confinement was severe.

Cave Entrance

Also known as The Hole or The Klondike, this method of punishment was the equivalent of burying someone alive. The inmate would be tossed into this hole and given only a slice of bread for sustenance. With the lack of nourishment and the limited supply of air, inmates often starved or suffocated before they were allowed back out.

Inmates were often sent to The Hole when they talked back or tried to fight with the guards. However, if they managed to escape from there, they had much worse punishments in store for them when they were caught.

The Iron Gag

The Iron Gag was the most torturous and deadly punishment, reserved for those who tried to break the solitary confinement rule by communicating with other inmates or for escaping The Hole. An iron collar was attached to the inmate's tongue, serving as the gag. The inmate's wrists were bound behind their back and attached to the iron collar around their tongue. If the inmate were to move their hands, the collar would tear into their tongue, causing it to bleed profusely.

This brutal punishment became the cause of death for many inmates, as it often resulted in severe blood loss.

The Water Bath

This punishment was most effective when disciplining escapees from The Hole's in the cold Pennsylvania winters. The Water Bath involved submerging an inmate in freezing water, then hanging them from a wall. By leaving the inmate in this state overnight, their skin would freeze until ice formed.

The Mad Chair

If the weather was too warm for The Water Bath, then The Mad Chair was another punishment available for those who escaped The Hole. The Mad Chair involved strapping an inmate to a chair as tight as possible, cutting off the circulation to their limbs. If left in this position long enough, there would be no choice but to amputate their limbs due to the lack of circulation.

Records of Casualties

Over the decades, meticulous records were kept and archived of the inmate populations, right down to each individual's characteristics. There are lists of what inmates did to be admitted to this prison and how long their sentences were. However, for how inmates died, there is no specific written evidence, which leads to much speculation about what exactly went on in Eastern State Penitentiary.

How many people lost their lives because of suffocation or starvation in The Hole? How many upset a warden one too many times, resulting in their untimely deaths at the hands of the guards? Better yet, did anyone record these deaths, or are there simply unmarked graves hidden somewhere on the property? Perhaps more insight can be gleaned from the accounts of some of the more memorable inmates.

Famous Penitentiary Criminals

Before the 1920s, the Eastern State Penitentiary housed petty criminals, aiming to reform those who committed minor crimes. However, the facility later took in more well-known names, intending to reform them as well.

Alphonse Capone

One of the most famous inmates at the Eastern State Penitentiary was Al Capone, a mob boss from Chicago. He was admitted to the prison in 1929 for carrying a concealed weapon and spent eight months there.

When night fell, Capone would cry out for a man named Jimmy, pleading for him to leave him be. Jimmy was believed to be Jimmy Clark, one of the seven people killed during the Valentine's Day Massacre, where members of one of Capone's rival gangs were shot to death. It was never officially confirmed that Capone was the mastermind behind the murders, but many speculated on his involvement.

Even after he left the prison, Jimmy continued to haunt him. Capone hired a psychic to help him get Jimmy to leave him alone, but nothing they did seemed to work. These hauntings, along with untreated syphilis eating at his brain for decades, inevitably led Capone to insanity at the end of his life.

William Sutton

William Sutton, also known as "Slick Willie," was an inmate at the Eastern State Penitentiary for eleven years. He was admitted to the prison in 1934 after attempting to rob the Corn Exchange Bank in New York. The media labeled him as the most well-known bank robber of the era, with over fifty successful bank and store robberies under his belt.

Sutton was most known, however, for his attempt to escape the prison in 1945. He and eleven other inmates made it out through a tunnel they dug, but shortly after reaching the surface, Sutton and the others were found and forced back to the prison.

Leo Callahan

Leo Callahan was admitted to Eastern State Penitentiary under the charge of Assault and Battery with Intent to Kill. Out of approximately one hundred inmates who attempted to escape from the prison, Callahan is credited as the only person who escaped from Eastern State Penitentiary and live to tell the tale.

In 1923, he planned an escape with five other inmates, and they scaled the prison's outer wall with a makeshift ladder. While his comrades were eventually caught, Callahan was the only one who never was. As a result, the rest of his life is a mystery, since he disappeared entirely from the public eye.

End of Service

After the prison's living conditions were deemed unacceptable in 1913, and due to overcrowding and the need to house more inmates, Eastern State Penitentiary officials decided it would be best to remove their solitary confinement rule. It became a congregate prison, where the inmates saw each other but were still not allowed to speak. The prison eventually closed its doors for good in 1971 after repairs became too expensive.

Ghost and Hauntings

The most popular claim about the Eastern State Penitentiary is that it is haunted, though the origins of this rumor are unclear. Now a famous tourist attraction, it was no wonder that the public turned its eye toward finding any traces of paranormal activity in that area. The allure of not knowing where it all began was enticing enough for people to flock to the area.

Hearing news of the punishments inmates faced, those who believed in the paranormal expected those tortured souls were still lurking in the prison, believing that they could not move on from their place of death. If these rumors were true, and it was possible to find proof of them, people would try their hardest to find it.

When the prison reopened its doors as a museum, it was only a matter of time before people came to investigate the rumors of the paranormal. Television shows that focused on finding and speaking to ghosts came to the museum in droves to skyrocket their ratings, while tourists came with their own equipment to satisfy their curiosity.

Eyewitness Encounters

Catwalk

One of the most well-known spots where people have reported witnessing these ghost encounters is the catwalk, a series of long corridors with an arched ceiling that overlooks the cellblocks from above. Visitors and tourists stated on multiple occasions that the temperature on the catwalk changes drastically, possibly indicating that a ghost is somewhere in the area. The television show Ghost Hunters recorded a video of a shadowy figure, helping to confirm the claims of passersby. One tourist even captured an audio recording of a man's voice saying, "I'm lonely."

Cellblock 12

Cellblock 12 is reportedly the most haunted section of the Eastern State Penitentiary. While it is currently a restricted area, it is no stranger to the shadowy figures that Blocks 4 and 6 also experience. Unexplained shadows resembling people were reportedly jumping from cell to cell on multiple occasions. There were also several people who stated they encountered someone running towards them at full speed, but who never reached them. Each version of this encounter differed slightly, but they were all in cellblock 12.

There is also an account of an unexplained figure in Civil War-era military clothing approaching an employee from behind in cellblock 12. At first, they thought the person was a coworker playing a prank on them, but the person was partially transparent upon closer inspection. Before the employee could examine or try to question the individual, they disappeared.

Phantom Voices

People have also claimed to encounter unexplained voices, such as screams or laughter. The words people heard were inaudible, but their intent seemed clear. Whispers aiming to send chills down the spines of visitors or workers had served their purpose, and giggles echoing down the hallways only further cemented the fear that people were being played with. It is commonplace for visitors to report feeling watched in these areas.

Gary Johnson Encounter

Gary Johnson was a locksmith who worked in the Eastern State Penitentiary in the early 1990s, helping to restore cellblocks that were once sealed behind rusted locks.

While removing a lock from Cellblock 4, Johnson states he was overwhelmed with a chilling, powerful energy that forced him into an out-of-body experience. During his supposed astral projection, he says he was dragged towards the cell and forced to witness the despairing remnants of hundreds of inmates who used to occupy it. Distorted images of people's faces and bodies danced on the walls. One of those figures even called out to Johnson, beckoning him to come even closer to the cell. Paralyzed with fear, Johnson most certainly did not.

There is a wide range of debate over what Johnson unleashed upon himself that day. The most common belief is that as he unlocked the cell, the ghosts of the cell's prior inmates could interact with him. When he was asked about this encounter years later, Johnson shuddered at the thought of what had happened in that cellblock.

This encounter took on a life of its own, spawning a multitude of theories and interpretations about what really happened to Johnson. No matter which version of the story, each always took place in Cellblock 4 and involved Johnson removing a lock. In some versions, there was no out-of-body experience, claiming Johnson was simply frozen in fear. Other versions claim a cold, spectral hand was shoved through his body. While each explanation has its differences, they are all still chilling.

Is Eastern State Penitentiary Haunted?

It's no surprise that when looking at the tales of Eastern State Penitentiary, one's first assumption could be that the place is haunted. Due to all the torture and death over the years the prison was active, people might believe in and imagine possible ghosts. But what other explanations could there be for what happened at the prison? Paranormal activity is intriguing because it cannot be confirmed. Is there a better explanation for what is happening at Eastern State Penitentiary?

What we know is that over fifty people took their own lives and at least a dozen others were murdered in this prison. These bodies were most likely not given proper burials, with some stating that some people were even buried alive. This disrespect for human life could lead some to believe that those lost souls are still lurking on the prison grounds.

However, while these accounts have reinforced the claims of paranormal activity since the 1940s, skeptics often say they walked through the prison and noticed nothing out of the ordinary.

To some, the Eastern State Penitentiary looks haunted. It's a crumbling structure that housed the brutal and gruesome deaths of a multitude of inmates. For those who believe in the supernatural, this information would be more than enough to conclude that the prison is haunted, but there is often more than one explanation.

Inconsistencies and Alternative Theories

Take, for example, the case involving Al Capone. While he claimed Jimmy haunted him, those screams into the night were not the only thing eating at him. His disease's origin is mostly unknown due to Capone's supposed refusal of treatment, but the syphilis that took root in his brain decades before never stopped harming him. In the last few years of his life, due to it being too late to treat his condition, it is reported that his brain was damaged enough to revert his mental state to that of a twelve-year-old.

It is unknown whether Capone's syphilis affected him during his stay in the penitentiary as much as towards the end of his life. However, knowing it was there at the time, the origin of his cries out toward Jimmy could be attributed to this illness.

Another unclear paranormal case is the one involving Gary Johnson. Johnson's descriptions seem far too vivid to have been fabricated on the spot, but since he was the only one to witness them, there is no support for his claim and one can only consider his testimony. However, when repeated by other people, the tale of Johnson's encounter is inconsistent. Each variation is terrifying in its own right, but these variations only make the case more unclear.

Unusual Working Conditions

Eyewitness cases do not always hold up when presented with evidence or even questioned for validity. Perhaps these are the main reasons people believe the prison is haunted: the people working there even reinforce the idea. The museum workers consider themselves to be working at a haunted site and advertise it as such for regular and seasonal events. They hold festivities around Halloween for this exact reason.

Not all workers at the museum have had encounters with the paranormal, but the ones they have reported are memorable. Some cases happened to people when they just started working at the museum, while others didn't experience these encounters until they had been there for months or years.

During the Halloween season, a pair of workers were the only ones remaining on the prison grounds when they heard unexplained sounds. These seemed to be coming from the room they were in, but there was no movement to be seen. The sound of papers and cups being shuffled around made the pair think the unexplained noises were close to them since they were cleaning art supplies.

One year, a visitor to the museum mailed back a bolt they stole from the facility. The visitor returned it to the museum hoping their streak of bad luck would stop. They explained in a letter sent along with the bolt that they were certain it was the cause of misfortune they experienced ever since stealing it.

A skeptical worker was sure that they didn't believe in paranormal activity, but they began to doubt their beliefs after working at the museum. They saw nothing happen, but specific parts of the museum gave them pains and chills: the punishment cells, a closet, and an office. No other area of the museum gave them these random bouts of uneasiness.

What Does it all Mean?

To trust these accounts of paranormal activity, you must first ask if you believe in them yourself. If you do, then your quest for answers could end there. You would have all the information you need, and you could join the more vocal crowd claiming the place is haunted.

But to solve the giant puzzle, one must look at its pieces first. To do so, one cannot look at the prison as a whole.

Anyone can fabricate paranormal evidence. When viewing television shows with recorded footage of disfigured ghosts or unexplained voices, there will always be the possibility that everything you are seeing is a result of movie magic.

There is only so much one can conclude without getting a hands-on view of the place. One way to get someone to decide whether or not they believe is by having them experience the prison's atmosphere themselves. Physical tours would be the best, but online tours could have a similar effect.

Eastern State Penitentiary may very well be haunted. With everything that has happened there during the 144 years it housed inmates, those who believe in the paranormal are likely to say the inmates are still there, haunting the place.

They point to the drastic changes in temperature in the catwalk area and the figures and voices people have encountered over the years when visiting the museum. However, these claims are made only by those who believe in ghosts. Those who do not believe in the paranormal have other questions when they think about this prison. How much of what is known is accurate, and could any of it be considered fabricated? Was Al Capone haunted by someone he ordered other people to kill or had his syphilis deteriorated his brain so much at that point that he was delusional? Did Gary Johnson have an out-of-body experience where he was beckoned to a cell by a horde of suffering spirits, or did he make up that story?

The lack of official death statistics raises many questions, mainly about the well-being of the inmates. We might surmise that people have died in this prison from the statements of employees and tourists alike. However, with the absence of recorded information about this subject, there is a possibility those death statistics are missing for a reason.

It is no question that this prison was home to questionable practices. The descriptions we have about the torture methods alone, along with the lack of death statistics, give the impression that these numbers have been hidden to avoid raising suspicion. Perhaps if the public knew just how many people had been dying in this prison, it would have been forced to close its doors long before.

These missing numbers also raise a different question: did they ever exist in the first place? How accurate is the prison's history, and what has been fabricated by the employees? Could the temperature changes on the catwalk result from physical influences, like air conditioners? Could the shadowy figures in the cellblocks be costumed employees hoping to find someone to target? Is every employee involved in some sort of fabrication to draw in tourists, working with each other to make it seem like ghosts are roaming the halls?

Even with this speculation, one cannot deny something is amiss in the Eastern State Penitentiary. The multitude of claims, each unique, makes the possibility of paranormal activity or some sort of intentional theatrics difficult to deny without other clear explanations. Whether genuine or fabricated, there is little proof of either.

Many wonder if the spirits of the inmates who lost their lives in the prison are still roaming its halls, waiting for an unsuspecting to approach. It would make sense for them to be angry. Their experience as an inmate in this prison had them scarred and left for dead. They never received closure for the torture they had to endure, so it's not hard to imagine their souls would still be in anguish. Like any other case of haunted activity, you can't be sure if something is real without looking into it yourself. If, after reading this chapter and drawing your own conclusions, if you are still uncertain, perhaps a visit of your own is in your future.

CHAPTER 6:
THE DARK HISTORY OF THE WHALEY HOUSE

T HE WHALEY HOUSE IS WIDELY CONSIDERED TO BE THE NUMBER one most haunted location in the United States. In the sunny city of San Diego, its history is a dark cloud over the beach-lined metropolis. Like the beginning of any paranormal story, darkness and mystery shroud the events surrounding this house. This location has a long history, with ties to ancient Native American burial sites and stories of this consecrated land. However, once the Whaley House was built, the dark past only continued to haunt this part of San Diego.

The Whaley House gained its name after the man who built the home, Thomas Whaley. He completed the construction in 1857, and the house has remained a famous tourist destination for a hundred years, with people from all over the world visiting the property. Today, there is a museum purpose-built to explore the history of this house. There is also a fascination with the haunted nature of the home, as many claim to have witnessed unexplainable happenings while there.

Dark History

The history of the Whaley House began long before the Whaley family even moved to the west coast. Near the Kumeyaay Native American settlement, the land where the Whaley House would eventually be built was once a gravesite for the mass killing of these native people. Whether they died from conflict or disease, the native community's numbers dwindled from 16,000 to 9,000 over ten years, resulting in the need for many graves. It is commonly theorized that any property built on top of Native American burial sites is in some way cursed, and this example is no exception.

The troubling history of this land only continued, with one of the most famous hanging cases in San Diego taking place right where the Whaley House would later be built. In August 1852, James Robertson—nicknamed Yankee Jim—was hanged for grand theft. In 1873, the Los Angeles Herald reported that officials thought him to be a dangerous man, and that he and his two accomplices had stolen a boat. After a quick trial, all three men were found guilty and sentenced to death by the gallows (Miller, 1873). With this many untimely deaths, it is easy to understand why some believe the Whaley House was always doomed for bad fortune. With the possibility of hundreds of unhappy and angry spirits trapped on the land, the dark history of this location could only continue and affect the next inhabitants.

The Whaley Family Home

Thomas Whaley was born in New York City in 1823, and was the second youngest of four siblings. His family ran a prominent gunsmith business, and after his father's death, his older brothers continued to run the company as locksmiths with much success. Thomas's life was one of privilege. He attended a boarding school in Connecticut, then The Washington Institute, before traveling to Europe to study for another two years. After completing his education and living the most of his life in New York, he considered his next steps.

He read in the newspaper that the west was prospering during the gold rush, and wanted to experience this for himself. He first moved to San Francisco, then to San Diego, which was much smaller in comparison. But Thomas enjoyed the European feel and comfortable climate, choosing to settle there. In 1853, Thomas married fellow east coaster Anna Eloise De Lannay in New York City and purchased a block of land on San Diego Avenue. There, he would begin constructing his family home (Strudwick, 1960, p. 19).

Even though he supposedly attended the hanging of Yankee Jim, Thomas found the history of the land unimportant in his decision making. In 1857, his home was complete. He built the house in the Greek Revival style, which was very popular in mid-nineteenth century America and considered modern for the time. It was built with heavy brick and high ceilings, and decorated with ornate embellishments. The design of the house considered the hot climate of Southern California, seeking to keep each room cool on hotter days (Strudwick, 1960, p. 7). This was a house built to stand the test of time.

Once the couple moved into their home, they began to hear the unexplained sounds of heavy footsteps that could not be attributed to anybody at the house. They described them like the steps of a heavier, older man. They soon accepted that this could be the spirit of Yankee Jim. Undeterred by this, Thomas opened a general store in the home. He was the offspring of a prosperous, sales-driven family, and had a keen eye for money and business. With this additional attachment, he further cemented the importance of the Whaley House both as his home and his means of financial success.

Thomas and Anna had six children: Francis Hinton, Thomas Junior, Anna Amelia, George Hay Ringgold, Violet Eloise, and Corinne Lillian. The tragedies the family experienced began shortly after their second child was born and would continue throughout the next generation.

Tragedies at the Whaley House

In January 1858, seventeen-month-old Thomas Junior died from scarlet fever. This was only a few months after Anna Amelia was born, and the family had only lived in their new home for less than a year. This death rocked the family. While they were in mourning, in August of that year, their brand new house and business erupted into flames. It wasn't the entire house that burned, though the store was utterly decimated, and certain parts of the living quarters damaged.

When Thomas saw the fire, he knew there was no way to save his store, though he managed to stop it from entirely engulfing the family home. This short burst of tragedies was a harrowing experience. Anna was still dealing with the loss of their son, and this second blow was almost too much for her to bear. Thomas suggested moving away, and Anna was pleased with this idea. With that, the Whaley's abandoned their life in San Diego and moved to San Francisco, where they had their final three children.

While the family was gone, Thomas entrusted the care of his home to Augustus S Ensworth. In 1862, Augustus wrote to the Whaley's informing them of the earthquake which had struck San Diego. "Many houses in town became cracked. I enclose a picture of your house, showing the cracks, but it looks worse on paper than it is. In fact the cracks are only discovered on inspection" (Strudwick, 1960, p. 28). Despite the letter claiming that the house was only minimally damaged, this was enough cause for Thomas and Anna to move the family back to San Diego.

Upon their arrival, Thomas completed repairs to the superficial damage caused by the earthquake and remodeled the home's interior to accommodate his now larger family. This remodeling also served another purpose, as Thomas created new business prospects inside the family home.

In 1868, he leased an upstairs bedroom, which he had converted into a theater. He leased it to Thomas W Tanner, who had a troupe of theatrical performers keen to use this space. This was the first commercial theater in San Diego. The room housed approximately 150 people, though it was largely standing room only. Once again, tragedy followed the Whaleys, as Thomas Tanner died only seventeen days after the theater opened and the troupe disbanded.

The next year, Thomas leased most of the upper floor, including three bedrooms, as a courthouse. As the house was in Old Town San Diego, this created an uproar for those who lived in New Town, as they wanted the courthouse to be nearer to them. The house, and the Whaley family, received much negative scrutiny, and even some attacks, as a result of this. Though Thomas attempted to sell the house to the county several times, the Whaley family remained the owners for many years to come.

In 1882, two of the Whaley children—Anna Amelia and Violet Eloise—married. Anna was in a happy marriage with her cousin John, who she considered the love of her life. Her sister was not as fortunate.

Violet reportedly experienced issues with her emotions, and at a young age found herself tied to a scam artist who married her with ulterior motives. His name was supposedly George T Bertolacci. In the beginning, it was a celebrated union. The family showered the couple with gifts and praise, enamored with the man who married their daughter, though this did not last long at all. Shortly after their union, Violet woke to find that George had fled. Despite being a married woman, she was all alone. It is believed that the con man was looking to secure a portion of the Whaley's fortune, and when this proved to be more difficult than he anticipated, he cut his losses and left his new bride to pick up the pieces of her life.

Unfortunately, this meant that Violet was forced to file for divorce, the proceedings of which took almost a full year to finalize. Even though her husband abandoned her, it was not commonplace for a divorce to occur at this point in history. It was particularly taboo that she had sought out the divorce, which led to her being shunned and isolated by her community. In 1885, at the young age of twenty-two, Violet Eloise Whaley shot herself in the chest. Her embarrassment and shame had not eased in the years since the failed marriage, and perhaps she saw suicide as her only way out. Her father found her shortly after, and she died in his arms.

She was the second of the Whaley children to pass away at the Whaley House.

At the time of Violet's suicide, her sister Corrine Lillian Whaley was engaged to be married. The death caused such controversy in the town that her fiancé broke the engagement off, citing that the scandal had caused too much reputational damage. Once again mourning a child and unable to stand the sight of their house, Thomas and Anna moved into a new home in San Diego and the Whaley House would remain vacant for nearly twenty years. In 1890, Thomas passed away after many years of failing health. He never returned to the home that he built.

In 1909, Francis—the eldest son and then the property owner— returned to fix the home. It had fallen into disrepair. He wanted to restore the house to its former glory so that he, his mother, and his siblings could live there again. In addition, Francis inherited his father's rental, theater, courthouse business and wanted to transform the home into a historical tourist attraction for visiting guests. He succeeded in his efforts, and the family returned for the final time to the Whaley House.

In 1913, Anna Whaley passed away, followed closely by Francis in 1914. Corrine Lillian was the last remaining family member in the home until she passed in 1953. Each of these three deaths occurred in the family home.

With all these untimely deaths and tragic occurrences, it is easy to understand why the Whaley family is considered to be doomed. However, this leads to a question: Did these tragedies happen to them because their home was cursed, or was this just an unlucky series of events that befell them through the course of their lives?

Paranormal Experiences

The popularity of the Whaley House is thanks to the sheer number of paranormal experiences people have had when visiting the home. It has been widely studied and reported on, from an investigation by *BuzzFeed Unsolved* to a visit by *The Travel Channel*. Those who have visited believe they have undoubtable proof that ghosts and spirits haunt this property. It is certainly the most famous haunted location in San Diego, and one of the most famous in the United States.

The property's history of hauntings dates back to before the Whaley tragedies, when the family still inhabited the home. As mentioned before, they often heard footsteps in the house that seemingly belonged to an older male and some witnessed the shadow of a bearded man walking through the house. Before his death, it is said that Thomas Junior would be found babbling and pointing to an unseen figure, even when he was alone in his room. While some believe this to be Yankee Jim, it is essential to remember that the house was built on top of a Native American graveyard, so it is possible that one of those spirits could also be the culprit of these sightings. Corrine, the last Whaley to die, also believed that she could sometimes feel her family members in the house with her. She rented some of the rooms out to boarders who corroborated her claims, advising that they too could hear and see spirits in the home.

The most popular sightings at the house are of the Whaley family members who died in the home. The baby, Thomas Junior, accounts for many of these experiences; people have reported hearing the noise of tiny infant footsteps, giggles, and chatter throughout the house. Sometimes, a baby can be heard crying from different rooms when there is no baby present. As Thomas Junior died a premature death, it is believed that his spirit is now trapped in his family home. He may not have been able to move to the other side peacefully, and may remain in his family home forever.

Sightings of Violet Eloise Whaley are also very common. Visitors have often reported seeing a distraught woman passing through the house, usually crying. She is also known to look lost and confused, unsure of what to do with herself. Once, there was an incident where the police were called to the Whaley House after reports of a woman screaming. When the police arrived, they saw a woman in the backyard, crying hysterically. An officer approached her and she stopped crying, looking up to smile at him. By the time he grabbed his flashlight and moved to shine it on her, she had disappeared. It is believed that this was Violet, as the location matched that of the place she shot herself, and the hysterical crying could only come from a paranormal being filled with despair.

Some have said that when in Violet's bedroom, they are overcome with a sense of sadness, sometimes to the point of tears. Once they are far enough from the room, the feeling disappears as quickly as it came, with no explanation. After her marriage fell apart, Violet shut herself away in that room to deal with her overwhelming grief alone, and it seems this grief permanently tainted the room. Violet's ghost appears to be quite prevalent at the Whaley House, as many attribute random cold spots and strange feelings to her. It is no wonder the spirit of Violet is trapped at the home, considering she experienced extreme depression in the years before her death, which led to her violently taking her own life. She may have been too distressed to move to the next realm, and it is possible that she does not realize she is dead, which could account for her confused appearance.

Many believe that they have witnessed the ghost of Anna, the mother, many times. Anna wore a distinct scent, and without knowing this, visitors have mentioned smelling a French perfume as they walked through the house. This has been attributed to Anna herself. She has also appeared to younger visitors, welcoming them into the home. She seems to be a friendly ghost who wants to make her house hospitable to those who come to it. Likely, Anna did not move on as she wanted to stay with her family, taking care of those still there. She had a difficult life, losing two children and her husband, attempting to keep the family afloat when tragedy struck them time and time again. In the afterlife, she may seek the peace that she never felt when she was alive.

Strangely, some have reported seeing the father, Thomas Whaley, at the house as well, though he did not die there. There have been accounts of him in his trademark coat and top hat, coming through the door. It is possible that he felt such a bond with the house and with his family that his ghost stayed with them as well.

However, there is no way to prove any of this.

Much like any typical ghost house, there are the traditional benchmarks for haunted homes. These include unexplained noises such as crying, laughing, and screaming, the sounds of footsteps when there is nobody present, objects moving on their own, the chandelier in the music room swinging back and forth, lights flickering, and cold spots that appear and disappear randomly.

There are also sightings of other ghosts haunting the house outside of the Whaley family. Some believe that a woman haunts the courthouse. Others have heard the sound of children playing who are not the Whaley's. Some say any nefarious behavior comes from those angered that the property was built on top of a graveyard.

The sheer number of ghosts at this house has turned even paranormal skeptics into believers, as it is nearly impossible to claim that this house does not have *something* strange about it.

A Tourist Destination

Since Francis Whaley himself set up the Whaley House to be a tourist destination, it only makes sense that the home is now one of the most popular sites to visit in Old Town, San Diego. The entire residence is now open as a museum, with visitors coming from all over the world to see recreations of how the Whaley family lived. It was formerly possible to walk through each room freely, though certain sections were blocked off in recent years, and artifacts have been encased in glass. Nonetheless, the experience still stands as one of the most intriguing in Southern California.

The Save Our Heritage Organization and the Natural Trust for Historic Preservation maintain the house. The aim is to preserve the home's history and show future generations what life in the late nineteenth century looked like. Some rooms are decorated as bedrooms, while others mirror the different business ventures of the Whaleys, such as the courthouse that once operated from within their home. A great deal of effort has been made to make this as historically accurate as possible, and it has created an excellent landmark for the city. Ghost tours are also run on the property. Those who partake highly rate these, as many are excited to see the most haunted home in America.

It will never be known if the Whaley family were just profoundly unlucky in life or genuinely cursed by their family home. However, this does not detract from how fascinating their story is and how popular their family home has become. For decades, this home has provided historical context and education to curious visitors, and the Whaley House has become an enduring part of San Diego's legacy.

CHAPTER 7:
THE TRUE STORY BEHIND THE MYRTLES PLANTATION.

SOME SCARY LOCATIONS ARE EVEN MORE FRIGHTENING BECAUSE OF THE truth that lies beneath the myth. Amid all the rumors and stories that shroud a location in mystery, there is a real story to be told. Whether this is a tale of murder, torture, or strange disappearance, the history is what adds to the intrigue of the supernatural and to the intrigue of what is really going on.

One tale that has a wild and exciting historical narrative is that of the Myrtles Plantation in St Francisville, Louisiana. Blanketed by the dark history of slavery in America, the Myrtles Plantation was home to at least ten murders that occurred in the main house (Taylor & Wiseheart, 2013). Now, it is regarded as one of the most haunted plantations in the United States.

Paranormal investigators have examined the plantation and the owners run many ghost tours throughout the property. Hundreds of people have witnessed strange, unexplainable happenings at the estate, and some even claim to have photographed ghosts and spirits residing on the premises.

This begs the question: Is the Myrtle Plantation really haunted, or are people just drawn to the stories that surround it? Additionally, we can consider what really happened at the plantation in its time as an operational estate and which ghosts supposedly stuck around.

Join me as we look into the stories of this interesting yet spooky location.

A Horrifying Past

There is no denying that American history is marred by centuries of slavery and mistreatment of its African American population. There is no way to brush past this when looking at the history of an operation plantation, and I do not intend to pretend that this did not happen. Instead, I seek to embrace the stories of those who suffered on the property and respect the past as best I can.

The history of the location begins long before the plantation was built. The story goes that this estate was constructed on a Tunica tribal burial ground (Nola Ghosts, 2021). In the supernatural world, any property built on a burial ground is cursed, so if a single murder happened at the plantation site, there was likely already paranormal activity afoot.

The plantation was built by General David Bradford in 1796, where he lived alone, in exile as penance for his role in the Pennsylvania Whiskey Rebellion—a protest against high taxes on whiskey which President Washington had to send troops in to break up (Nola Ghosts, 2021). Due to this dalliance, Bradford was mostly known around town as Whiskey Dave. Once he was pardoned, his wife, Elizabeth, and their children moved to join him on the property.

The property was built in the style of a traditional Louisiana plantation, with a clapboard exterior and a large veranda stretching across the entire house. Inside, the house has twenty-eight rooms over two floors and lavish carvings and ornaments both inside and out. It has an enormous chandelier hanging in one of the halls, and two parlors feature marble mantels. There is no denying the property was built to be marveled at by all those who saw it. To this day, it is still a stunning structure with many of the features of the original house preserved.

The plantation was later sold in 1817 to Elizabeth and David's daughter, Sara, and her husband, Clarke Woodruff. Whilst the Bradford family was in control of the plantation, it was called *Laurel Grove*, though the name changed to the *Myrtles Plantation* when Ruffin Gray Stirling and his wife Mary Catherine Cobb later took ownership. They renamed the property after the crape myrtle that grew there (Cellania, 2009). The property

was sold and bought many times over its history and saw several families come and go.

As the house switched owners, the enslaved people on the property were sold as a part of the property. When Clarke and Sara took control, they "expanded the holdings of the plantation and planted about six hundred and fifty acres of indigo and cotton" (Harrington, 2020). The couple had three children, Cornelia Africa Gale, James, and Mary Octavia (Taylor & Wiseheart, 2013).

Clarke allegedly had an affair with an enslaved person named Chloe, with whom he had a tumultuous history. Legend says that Chloe became paranoid that Clarke would end their relationship, so she began eavesdropping on his conversations. When she was caught, Clarke saw to it that her ear was cut off, and she subsequently wore a scarf to hide what had happened to her (Cellania, 2009). There is also a rumor that claims Chloe once poisoned a cake for the birthday celebration of one of Clarke and

Sara's children. Clarke did not eat the cake, "but his wife and children did and subsequently died" (Cellania, 2009). The other slaves, perhaps afraid that their owner would punish them also, dragged Chloe from her room and hanged her from a nearby tree."

An alternative story to the history of the Woodruff family is that they passed away from yellow fever. This one is more widely believed by historians, though fans of the paranormal tend to lean towards the story of vengeful poisoning.

Official historical records show one recorded murder on the property. The victim's name was William Drew Winter, an attorney who lived on the property from 1865 until 1871. He was shot, seemingly at random, by a stranger on the front porch and staggered into the home. He tried to climb up the stairs, calling for help, though he succumbed to his injuries on the seventeenth step (Haunted Rooms, 2018).

Despite records not showing any further murders, there is a long-standing assumption that many more violent deaths occurred on the plantation. Perhaps these deaths were not registered or the owners of the property falsified documentation. There is no way of knowing exactly what happened, which has caused speculation about what could have happened at the plantation.

The history of this old property is rich and troubled. Many families passed through the doors, and many people took their final breaths there. With many violent and difficult deaths occurring there, it is no wonder that the stories of hauntings and the paranormal have taken over the history of the plantation.

So, what is haunting the Myrtles Plantation? How many ghosts roam the halls of the property, and what have people seen when visiting?

Hauntings and Encounters

The Myrtles Plantation is allegedly so haunted that people from all over the world travel for the chance to run into a ghost. It's almost impossible to name every single spirit that has been sighted at the plantation. People have been visiting for years, and many have attempted to capture what they have witnessed on camera. Though as always, capturing photographic or filmed evidence of the supernatural is difficult.

The plantation has been host to many paranormal researchers and ghost hunters in the last few decades. This includes a team from the Travel Channel who investigated the story of the poisoned children and attempted to capture their ghosts on camera (Belanger, 2014).

With all these eyewitnesses who swear they saw something supernatural, one may wonder: Who roams the plantation? Where are they spotted? What sightings have there been?

The Ghost of William Drew Winter

As mentioned before, the only recorded murder on the plantation was that of William Drew Winter, who's death was exceedingly violent. It is no surprise that his ghost is said to have remained on the property and visitors often claim to see him. Legend has it that his footsteps can still be heard on the stairs where he passed away. Many, hearing noises on the stairs, think someone is climbing up behind them, but there is nobody there.

Some claim the noise sounds like someone thumping and staggering up the stairs, which is in line with how Winter spent his last moments alive. The sound is more prevalent at night, and sometimes people have even heard someone begging for assistance in this exact location. A few visitors have even claimed to see William on the stairs, though this seems to be a frightening experience. He is said to appear as a dying man, after all.

Like with any ghost story, there is an element of mythology that changed the narrative over time. Some claim that William Winter never actually made it to the stairs of the home, rather dying right away on the porch (Harrington, 2020). This means that any noises heard on the stairs are either figments of peoples' imaginations, or perhaps another spirit altogether.

Regardless of what you believe, a glimpse of William's ghost would undoubtedly be a sight to see. He is one of the most sought-after spirits, and people spend time near the staircase just hoping that he will make an appearance.

The Legend of Chloe

The story of Chloe poisoning the Woodruff family is the most famous and well-known tale that comes from the Myrtles Plantation. She supposedly distilled extract from oleanders that grew nearby and baked them into a cake for the children. While she did not manage to kill her punisher and former lover, Clarke Woodruff, she murdered his two daughters and his wife. She was hanged for her crimes sometime around 1823. Some say she is now doomed to haunt the property for the rest of eternity.

Some people have told stories of Chloe taking their items. Most notably, she'll steal an earring from a pair that belongs to women staying at the plantation—she only needs one due to her ear being cut off. Some see Chloe at night in the bedrooms, visiting as they sleep. Those who have been lucky enough to wake up and see her have found her to be calm and not frightening at all. Despite her murderous history when she was alive, she seems to be an incredibly peaceful ghost who is just curious about the living. Those who have encountered her say she has traditional Southern manners and just wants to see who is inhabiting the plantation.

Supposedly, a photographer was even able to catch Chloe on camera. This man was surveying the property for insurance purposes, taking photos as part of his standard procedure. He swears he did not see anybody before taking a particular picture, and was shocked to find that a person had appeared in his photo afterward (Nola Ghosts, 2021). Many believe this story because the surveyor was not visiting the property seeking a supernatural encounter, and seemed very shocked by what they saw.

The plantation now sells a very popular postcard with this image on the front. It is blurry, but there is a chance that someone was standing in the field, captured in a supernatural photo.

People are sure that this is a woman who once lived on the property—even if it's not Chloe herself—because those who have spotted her say she bears an uncanny resemblance to a painting that hangs at the plantation. Some claim to have clearly seen her staring through windows, her features plainly visible to the naked eye.

The Woman in the Green Turban

There is an unnamed ghost that has supposedly appeared to a few guests and has given them quite a fright. This is the ghost of an African American woman in a green turban and a long dress. While guests are sleeping in a downstairs bedroom, they have woken up to see this woman standing silently at the foot of their bed. She is frequently seen holding a candlestick which appears so real it emits a strong glow and even heat from the flame. She has reportedly lifted mosquito nets from the beds to peers in at the occupants. Some guets have said she even reached out to touch them, though she has never been reported as being violent or hurting anyone.

Some have attempted to figure out who this woman is, attributing her presence to either an enslaved woman or a governess who lived on the property and who was likely mistreated. According to her myth, and similar to the story of Chloe, she had her ears cut off, which is why she is seen wearing a turban. Those who have had a better look at the apparition have even noticed a scar near her hairline.

The story says she had her child was removed from her care, and this is who she is looking for when wandering the bedrooms of the lower floor. "She has been seen peering into the faces of sleeping guests, presumably still looking for her lost child" (Harrington, 2020).

Due to the similarities with her injuries and appearance, some believe that this could actually be Chloe. Most people familiar with the ghosts are adamant that these are two different entities. However, there is no way to know for sure. It is entirely possible that two different women could have experienced the same punishment in their time at the plantation. The years of slavery were incredibly cruel, and slave owners would use the same kinds of mutilations and retributions to hurt their slaves.

Visitors have become fascinated with seeing this woman, especially because she is friendly. People have spent hours in the lower bedrooms hoping that she will come and see them, though she is selective with whom she visits.

What the Residents Have Experienced

There have been several residents and long-term employees of the plantation who have experienced many encounters with the supernatural. They all have fascinating stories of the occurrences they experienced. Some were frightened, while others had peaceful interactions, but all were left fascinated by what they experienced at the Myrtles Plantation.

Frances Kermeen Myers

Frances Kermeen Myers and her husband James moved to the Myrtles Plantation in the 1970s and operated a bed and breakfast from the property. The couple went through so many haunting experiences while living there that Frances even wrote a book called *Myrtles Plantation: The True Story of America's Most Haunted*

House (Kermeen, 2005). During their years there, they claim to have experienced non-stop hauntings and paranormal experiences, describing the typical signs of a haunted house: unexplained footsteps, random voices when there was nobody in the room, lingering perfume that belonged to nobody in the house, and strange noises that echoed through the house at all hours of the night. Sometimes, they would even hear a baby crying when no infants were staying at the plantation. Notably, Frances had a few encounters with the lady in the green turban. She found her at the foot of her bed and even felt her touch a few times.

Frances also reported the presence of Chloe and William Winter at the plantation. She told stories in podcasts and interviews the experiences of her bed and breakfast guests while staying at the plantation, including reports of beds floating above the ground and items flying across rooms. "I had thousands of reports from guests in my ten years there, from hearing things, seeing things, the bed lifting and floating around the room, to being chased down the stairs with a broom," (Carter, 2017).

The Moss Family

After nearly a decade living at the property, the Kermeen-Myer family had enough of the constant hauntings and sold the property to John and Teeta Moss, the current owners of the plantation. When they first moved into the property, they knew it had a history of hauntings but weren't sure that they believed it to be true. They thought it could be a marketing scheme made up to drum up visitor numbers. "For the first seven years, the couple and their two sons lived on the top floor of the mansion while the bottom continued as a bed and breakfast for traveling guests" (Wood, 2018). Teeta says that within two weeks, the family was already experiencing high levels of supernatural events. She would hear her husband's voice in the house when he wasn't on the property, and sometimes they heard the voice of a childhood friend. One paranormal expert explained that sometimes spirits have the power to mimic voices that make the living comfortable, to show they are not dangerous.

The most startling event to happen to the Moss family came in 1993 and involved Morgan Moss, their son, who was only ten-and-a-half months old at the time. Morgan was asleep in an antique bed with iron railings while Teeta was in the office finalizing details for the property's restaurant. She was alone when she heard a raspy voice say, "Check your baby." At first, she assumed her mind was playing tricks on her and ignored it, going back to work. When it happened again, she decided it was worth checking out. When she arrived in the bedroom, she saw her son was missing from his crib. She ran through the house screaming and looking for him, only to find him making his way toward the edge of the pond outside. She reached him and held him in her arms, terrified and wondering what could have happened to him if she hadn't gone to check.

"When I held him, a warm blanket enveloped the two of us—so real that I could feel the fabric and warmth. Then that same voice said to me, 'You need not worry, your family will never be harmed here'" (Wood, 2018). From that day, Teeta looked at the ghosts and spirits as the family's guardians.

The Moss family claims to have often seen the ghosts of playing children on the premises, including seeing Chloe roaming between the buildings on the plantations. Teeta says she captured a picture of Chloe. While there is no solid evidence of Chloe ever existing, this apparition is proof enough for many that she lived on the property.

Hester Eby

Hester Eby has been the director of tourism at the plantation for over thirty years, and has reported countless supernatural sightings. Just like Teeta, she believes the ghosts are harmless. An incident she says she will never forget is the first time she saw the ghost of a little girl at the property.

Two guests arrived and asked to purchase two tickets to gain entrance, and Hester asked if they also wanted a ticket for their daughter. They laughed and told her they never had children, but she saw them walking up the driveway with a little girl. She remembered all the details of the child and was even going to comment to the couple about how cute a child she was. Hester says of the child, "She had long blonde hair and was dressed in an antique white dress skipping behind her mother," (Wood, 2018). Hester was surprised the girl had simply disappeared, and once she allowed the guests admission into the property, she walked back outside to look for her. The little girl appeared again and said hello, then giggled and disappeared again. It was like she was playing a game with Hester.

Hester also claims to have seen uniformed soldiers standing at the foot of the main staircase that could be ghosts from the Civil War. She says all her interactions with the ghosts have been lovely. She's enjoyed being around the spirits and has never had any issues. Hester mentioned they can be a bit cheeky and misbehave at times, but she says that just adds to the joys of working at the plantation.

Other Paranormal Sightings

Other than the named ghosts at the Myrtles Plantation, a myriad of additional paranormal sightings and activities have been reported by many. Hester Ebby isn't the only person who has seen soldiers around the house. During the Civil War, Union soldiers came to the plantation and attempted to loot the property. They were unsuccessful, as Confederate soldiers were alerted of their presence and came to shoot three of them dead. Years later, a maid attempted to clean the blood which had stained the floors of the hall but was unable to get it clean. It was like it was stuck there permanently. Now, people believe they witness these soldiers lying in this exact spot on the first floor, in a pool of their blood.

There are also often sightings of two little blonde girls peeking through different windows at the plantation. Some assume these apparitions are the two Woodruff girls who died there.

Finally, there are the classic signs of a haunted house. There are often strange orbs photographed, and people see things moving with no explanation. "A mirror in the hallway reportedly shows faces of the dead from time to time" (Cellania, 2009). No matter how many times it is cleaned, there is no getting rid of the supernatural history of the plantation.

Are Any of These Stories Real?

There are so many sightings and sounds that point towards the property being haunted that people visit hoping to witness the paranormal. However, as with any of these haunted locations, skeptics are sure nothing is happening.

Many of the reasons non-believers have doubts are because no ghost stories have beFen proven true by concrete evidence. For example, there is no reason to believe that an enslaved person called Chloe ever existed or lived at the house. Sure, the plantation has a horrific history as part of the slave trade and people there were owned like property, but there is no historical documentation that shows a woman with this name ever lived there. It is also entirely possible that Clarke Woodruff had an affair with an enslaved person, however; there is no reason to believe that this person poisoned his children and his wife. In fact, looking at this time in history, it is more likely that they died from scarlet fever. Skeptics believe this story was started to spook visitors at the plantation and grew into a broader legend that couldn't be stopped. Now, it is passed down from visitor to visitor, and people are desperate to see the supposed ghost of the murderous Chloe.

Another debunked story is that of the Union soldiers. Surviving members of the Woodruff family say that this is absolutely not true and that there were no visits from soldiers during the Civil

War. The story of three men being shot is just a fantasy made up to add to the mystery of the property.

The only documented and confirmed death is that of William Drew Winter. However, skeptics do not believe that his ghost still roams the halls of the plantation. They believe that owners of the property have either seen shadows that have led them to believe there is someone there and that the sounds of footsteps are purely the creaks of an old house.

At the end of the day, without experiencing the paranormal themselves, it is improbable that a skeptical person will change their mind. Even if they do witness something supernatural, they will likely explain it away with logic and reason.

Ghosts or Something Else?

It is up to you to decide whether you believe the stories of the Myrtles Plantation ghosts. If you are a skeptic, perhaps you are not convinced by the numerous eyewitness accounts, or perhaps there is nothing that can show you that any of this is true.

Whatever your opinion, you cannot deny that these stories are fascinating.

Nowadays, the plantation has embraced its history and the supernatural stories. The website openly promotes its reputation as one of the most haunted places in America and encourages ghost hunters and believers alike (The Myrtles Plantation, 2022). They run tours, and guests visit from all over hoping to run into a spirit. The bed and breakfast is also still operational, and many rooms are named after the previous owners.

If you think about the stories told, you can likely perceive why this is such a highly toured location. The opportunity to be visited by Chloe or the Lady in the Green Turban is exciting. Hearing the footsteps of William Winter would be quite a surprising experience, and seeing any of the children who roam the plantation would be thrilling.

No matter where you stand on the supernatural, the story and history that comes from the Myrtles Plantation are unforgettable. Now it's up to you to decide what is real and what is fake.

CHAPTER 8:
WHAT'S HAUNTING THE SALLIE HOUSE?

THE SALLIE HOUSE IN ATCHISON, KANSAS, IS A NINETEENTH-CENTURY house that reportedly became haunted by the ghost of a little girl named Sallie after her untimely death there. Of course, some have questioned the validity of this. Paranormal experts have said something unexplainable is happening on this property, while skeptics have diminished this as pure nonsense. Despite this conflict of opinions, the Sallie House is widely regarded as one of the most haunted places in America, with thousands of visits from tourists seeking a paranormal experience (Lawrence, 2017).

Who Is Sallie?

The story of Sallie begins with Doctor Charles Finney. The Finney family moved to the Sallie House — as it would come to be known — in the 1870s. The doctor opened his practice there, including examination rooms. The front of the house served as office space, and the upstairs as the family living quarters.

One day, Doctor Finney heard his neighbor screaming for help before coming to the house for assistance. They were carrying their daughter and begging for the doctor to intervene. Finney surmised the girl had a ruptured appendix and immediately operated on her. Reportedly, he did not have time to make it to his examination rooms. Instead, the operation took place in his kitchen. The girl was set down, thrashing and screaming; but before the doctor could begin the procedure, he needed to sedate her. He eventually got her sedated enough to lie still.

This took so long that valuable time was lost, and in the subsequent rush, Finney did not realize the girl was still wide awake during the surgery. Thus, she felt everything as he operated. Unfortunately, she died from the shock of the surgical pain and extreme blood loss.

The deceased young girl was named Sallie, and it is theorized that her spirit haunts the house to this day. Conflicting reports claim that Sallie's surgery and resulting death happened in the basement, where Doctor Finney traditionally consulted and operated. This is a popular theory, as the basement of the house has been said to be one of the most haunted spots on the premises. However, there is no evidence of either surgery in historical documentation, so there is no way to say for sure the event even occurred.

There is little to no proof that Sallie was a young girl in Atchison at all. No records show that a girl died in the Finney house, and journalists Fahrlander and Vickers report anthropologist Sean Daley as saying there was never a young girl by that name who lived in the town. He asserts that there was no paranormal activity associated with the house until the 1990s, though even he has witnessed unusual and unexplained activity on the property. He does not claim that it is impossible that the house is haunted, just that there is no proof of Sallie's existence. However, this could be because her life and death documentation may have been lost in the many years since, or because her family was poor and never documented her at all. Of course, nineteenth century record-keeping was not nearly as advanced or thorough as it is now.

The last Finney of the family lived in the house until 1947, when it was sold and passed onto new owners.

People have reported many stories about Sallie over the years. She was first thought to be a peaceful spirit, but there have been stories of visitors leaving the house with scratches and bruises. These acts of violence are viewed by some as being demonic in nature and have added to the celebrity of the Sallie House. Nonetheless, unexplained movements have been reported, like stuffed toys moving on their own and photos being turned upside down. For those who have visited, it is undeniable that something strange is happening at the Sallie House.

The Pickmans

While the ghost of the Sallie House has a long history, the story gained popularity in the 1990s when the Pickman family moved in. Newlyweds Debra and Tony Pickman moved into the house in 1993, while Debra was pregnant with their son. At first, things seemed perfectly normal in their new home. Their lives were very exciting; they were blissfully anticipating the birth of their first child. There was nothing out of the ordinary until something attacked Tony in his own home. While the Pickmans had noticed unusual events in their home before the attacks began, it was only afterward that they understood there was another entity in their home.

It is important to note that the Pickmans' experience in the Sallie House was so harrowing it drove Debra to write a book about it, titled *The Sallie House Haunting: A True Story*, where she chronicles the family's ordeal with the spirit residing in their home. Debra includes passages from her journal from this time and photos of their lives, attempting to prove that they experienced a ghost living with them. A lot of her first-hand experience informs our knowledge of the goings-on in this house. In addition to this, the family has spoken publicly about their ordeal. Debra and Tony's story has been read by hundreds of people worldwide and has enticed many to research the paranormal. Having a first-hand account of something so strange makes it easier to understand how these things occur.

Debra writes that while she was a paranormal believer long before the events at the Sallie House, her husband was not. Tony was incredibly skeptical and would not easily believe that the house was haunted. However, over the two years they lived in the home, Tony no longer claimed skepticism as his perception of spirits and demons changed forever. The Pickmans have since become paranormal researchers and have spoken at conferences about their experiences.

Abnormal Behavior

Before any attacks started, the Pickmans noticed abnormal behavior in the house. Certain spots in the home were often freezing with no explanation for the temperature drop. The house did not have any centralized air conditioning, so the change struck them as very odd.

Debra speaks specifically about the first time the presence of another being truly shook her. On a hot night in the third trimester of her pregnancy, a blood-curdling scream awakened her. Then, she heard the sound of someone running down the stairs of the house. In her sleepy haze, she assumed someone had broken into the home and attempted to sit up, but what felt like a heavy object struck her in the face. This chilled her to the bone, and she screamed as well, waking Tony, who was sleeping next to her. Once awake, Tony also started screaming, though it was unclear if he was attacked as well. They did not stop until they realized they had no idea what they were screaming about (Pickman, 2010, p. 25).

The Pickmans also noticed that technology in the home did not work as designed, particularly in the kitchen. For example, the time displayed on their oven would inexplicably change, and digital timers they set would malfunction. They began to make special note of this, paying close attention to how the times would vary and found the clocks would go from displaying four minutes left to fourteen minutes and back again.

Additionally, there were of course the classic hallmarks of a haunted house. There was unexplained stomping through the house, knocks, and thuds when there was no one present, and the sounds of furniture moving. Dogs would bark at nothing, and cats would become suddenly frightened and run out of the room. Cold spots continued to appear at random, and the Pickmans would even feel someone brush past them from time to time.

Once the Pickmans' son was born, paranormal activity began to centralize in his room. Toys would be moved from their spots and the bedroom light would switch on randomly. A neighbor once asked the Pickmans why they kept the light on in the nursery all the time, especially as they had a small baby living in the house. This baffled them, as they turned it off every night. Their son, a happy baby, would often be found playing on his own, smiling and babbling into thin air as though he were talking to someone. They would sometimes hear the baby giggling while alone. Debra once found his toys arranged in a circle in the middle of the room. Neither she nor her husband had created this formation. This incident caused an uneasy feeling, and they cleaned up the toys, switched off the light, and went downstairs.

When checking on the child later, they were horrified to find the light was on again. Also, a stuffed bear was back on the floor where the circle had been. As their son was a newborn and there were no other people in the house, it made no sense how this had happened.

The first sighting of a ghost came from Tony, who claims that he saw a young girl in the home wearing an 1800s-style white dress. The presence confused him, but could not deny what he saw with his own eyes. The first place he ever spotted her was the kitchen — the suspected location of Sallie's untimely and painful death. He ran to his wife, pale-faced, and frantically told her he had seen something, then sketched out a picture of a girl. This drawing made its way to a neighbor, who commented that his house's former residents had a daughter whose imaginary friend was named Sallie. Later, this girl confirmed the drawing strongly resembled her friend.

Around this same time, Debra convinced Tony that they needed to bring a psychic to the house to help them figure out what was happening. Tony was previously hesitant, but at that time conceded and a psychic came to visit. The local psychic sensed a young girl named Sallie, who had died on the property and was especially comfortable in the nursery as she felt the safest there. The Pickmans agreed with this assertion, as they had often had paranormal experiences there. The Pickmans and their friends and neighbors would refer to the ghost as Sallie from that day on.

The Attacks

Debra and the baby were spared from any attacks by the ghost, while Tony suffered the most. Some suspect that Sallie only attacked men, as her death purportedly came at the hands of Charles Finney. She likely blamed men for how she died and would take her revenge on any male that visited the home. She perhaps felt unsafe in their presence and would therefore lash out. Sallie's other activity, such as moving objects, were entirely peaceful, and her attacks would only come when she seemed to be angered or disturbed. As she was so young at the time of her death, this made her particularly dangerous and unpredictable. It is believed in the paranormal community that young ghosts are the most powerful.

The Pickman family experienced many disturbing things in the two years that they lived in the Sallie House, though Tony bore the brunt of any violence. This began with Tony being repeatedly scratched by an unseen force. This happened so many times that he caught it on camera, where it was clear that nothing was touching him, yet marks and scratches appeared on his body. This would often happen when he was either entering or leaving the house, sometimes finding himself bruised by the force of the attack. If another male were to visit, they would sometimes experience the same sensation. Tony would ignore the girl, not acknowledging when she became present, hoping this would stop the attacks—but this often had the opposite effect. Debra tells one story of Sallie biting Tony on the back of the thigh. He had been alone, lying on the couch in the living room, when this took place. The resulting wound could not otherwise be explained, as their son was only a few months old with no teeth.

There is also a story of Tony waking up after hearing people in the house whispering through the walls. He felt a surge of panic and was unable to move, paralyzed in his bed. The whispers grew louder and louder and became more frantic, until suddenly he felt as though he were being strangled. Then, after a few moments, the sensation disappeared, as did the noises.

If people attempted to visit the Pickmans' basement, bricks would sporadically come flying towards them as if someone were throwing them. There has been no conclusive explanation as to why this happens. However, this also adds weight to the theory that Sallie died in the basement. Her apparent refusal to allow anybody to visit this spot could prove that she was looking to guard it against anyone, perhaps so that they would not suffer the same pain she once did.

Some people have been critical of the Pickmans' behavior towards Sallie, claiming that they invited her in and made her feel welcome rather than trying to deter the ghost. It is reported that they gave her gifts, kept out toys which she liked, and left lights on in rooms to keep her comfortable. Perhaps they thought this would keep the ghost at peace and less likely to hurt them or destroy their belongings. The ghost had something to play with by leaving out toys and would not need to amuse itself in other ways. Despite attacking Tony and their visitors, the Pickmans wanted to make peace with this entity in their home.

Ghost of a Young Girl or a Demon?

Some of the more unusual parts of the story of the Sallie House are the reports of how dangerous and physically violent the spirit could be. Often, elements of the attacks on the Pickmans seemed more demonic than ghost-like. Aside from the attacks on Tony, the ghost would ignite fires out of nowhere, which is typically a sign of something much darker than an average haunting. Along with this, photos would be turned upside down, and reports of objects both levitating and moving on their own have led some to believe that something more sinister was happening in this house.

Despite what the Pickmans and others saw, there is still reason to believe that the Sallie House could be haunted by a demon rather than the innocent ghost of a young girl. This demon could be masquerading as a sweet little girl rather than this being Sallie herself. Some of the Pickmans' testimony about this time could go a long way to support this idea. For example, they complained they often smelled something foul in the house and could not find the source. They described it as a scent of burning sulfur. It is widely believed that the presence of a demon can be identified by such a smell, with theorists attributing the smell of sulfur to hell and dark spirits (Kroonenberg, 2013).

Psychics who have visited the house have had varied experiences and reported different findings. Some have determined that the spirit is, in fact, a seven-year-old girl who complains of pain and discomfort around her stomach and abdomen, and who does not seem violent. They believe that this is not a harmful spirit, but rather a trapped soul who died an untimely death. Others have found the exact opposite, advising that the house had a very dark presence and that it was feeding off the terror and anxiety inflicted upon the living. The spirit or demon was found mainly around the back of the home and in the basement where the brick attacks occurred. They believe the demon was there to cause harm.

Much evidence has been gathered over the years from the Sallie House. This includes photos and videos of paranormal activity. For example, one picture that supports the demon theory exhibits the silhouette of a young girl standing at a window with a horned demon behind her. This is viewed by some as proof that the demon is impersonating an innocent child for its sinister acts.

A decade after leaving the house, the Pickmans returned with a team of paranormal investigators to assess the property. Once again, Tony became the target of an attack and was thrown back about four feet and pinned to the ground, unable to get up. The investigators called out, "In the name of God, let him go." At this, he was released.

Nonetheless, the Pickmans maintain the ghost wasn't necessarily a demon, as they remained there even with a very young baby. They would have left immediately if their son had been threatened, and he never was. The Pickman family also have said that the ghost they saw did not look frightening; they found her to look sweet or innocent. However, this does not prove that it was not a demon, as some argue it could have taken any form to achieve its goal.

So, what is haunting the Sallie House? Is it the ghost of a frightened young girl whose life was cut short, or something much more sinister? There is also speculation that the Pickmans made up much of this story, seeking to capitalize on the fame and make some fortune. Skeptics view Debra's book as proof of this, as well as the Pickmans' presence in paranormal circles, their speaking appearances, and their many interviews about their time in the home. However, even if the Pickmans financially gained from their experience, some find it difficult to deny the validity of the evidence they collected over the two years they lived there.

Visiting the Sallie House

It is now possible to visit the Sallie House in Atchison and experience the haunting yourself. As the house is believed to be so heavily haunted by a ghost who is sometimes violent, visitors must sign a waiver in case of injury. While there have been no confirmed attacks on guests since 1993, every precaution is taken to ensure that those in the house remain safe during their time there. Not only can you tour the Sallie House during the day, but you can also book to stay overnight and have the entire experience of the haunting. This has become a popular option for thrill-seekers and fans of the paranormal, especially around Halloween, when ghost activity is said to be at an all-time high.

The best part about visiting the Sallie House is drawing your own conclusion about what is happening on the premises.

Visitors can decide whether they think something dark resides there, or that the tale has all been made up to encourage further visitors.

CONCLUSION

MANY FIND STORIES OF HAUNTINGS AND PARANORMAL ACTIVITY LIKE these to be interesting no matter their stance on the validity of the claims. Even those skeptical of spirits and the supernatural might find entertainment in the history behind the myths. By examining these stories, it is clear that over the course of history, people have vehemently believed in the paranormal. Some of these events are so difficult to explain that some find it hard to believe anything else. In each of these stories, people experience terrible misfortunes. Often there is an untimely and gruesome death, and frequently entire families are involved in the horrors. From the Perelsons to the Whaleys, families all over America have been through dark events which have not been forgotten.

It is clear in these stories that the cause of death and circumstances of tragedy relate to claims of paranormal experiences that follow. Sallie died a painful and untimely death. Therefore, she took out her rage on men who visited the home. Demon or not, the reason behind her targeted attacks seems obvious. A person who did not die a painful death, like Anna Whaley, proves to be a more welcoming ghost. Anna invites guests into her home, looking to make them comfortable. Anna's life was marred with tragedy and she grieved the death of two of her own children, so her spirit is overcompensating for what she lost in her life.

The screams of Lillian Perelson are loud, as her husband unexpectedly attacked her. The playful nature of Jackie on the Grey Ghost shows that a young spirit may not recognize what has happened to them, as she is often heard calling for her parents or singing to passersby. The story of Anna Ecklund shows how abuse and other horrific acts can lead to unexplained behavior, in her case leading those around her to believe that she was possessed by the devil. History and stories of the paranormal are intricately entwined. Everything we suspect about the supernatural comes from this history, which should not be forgotten.

The best thing about looking back on history is learning from it, which is precisely why some of the horrible practices found throughout these stories no longer happen. Surgeries for children are a lot safer, the conversation around mental health is more prevalent, women are no longer shunned for being divorced, safety on large ships is well monitored to prevent drownings and accidents, and exorcisms have been outlawed. While we read about these stories with great interest, we should also learn from them.

Thank you very much for joining me on this journey as I reflect on some of the best ghost stories in America. I hope that you have enjoyed exploring the haunted locations, paranormal encounters, and demonic possessions with me.

JOURNEY'S END

AS WE CONCLUDE OUR THRILLING ODYSSEY THROUGH "GHOST STORIES: The Haunted Locations and Paranormal Encounters Bundle," I, H.J. Tidy, want to express my deepest gratitude for joining us on this captivating adventure. I hope you have truly enjoyed this collection of haunting tales and ghostly encounters.

In "Ghost Stories Vol I," we ventured into the unknown depths, bearing witness to the haunting mystery of the Brown Lady of Raynham Hall, uncovering the dark secrets of the infamous Roosevelt Hotel, and facing the bone-chilling encounter with Robert the Doll. These undeniably strange stories prompt us to contemplate the eerie possibility of the paranormal world causing harm and raising questions about its existence.

Continuing into "Ghost Stories Vol II," you immersed yourself in eight unique and spine-tingling tales of paranormal encounters worldwide. Among them, you uncovered the most incredible ghost story in American history, drawn into the chilling tale of The Bell Witch. This enigmatic and evil spirit has plagued generations with terror. Additionally, you delved into the unfortunate events of one of the most famous true crime stories of the 20th century, encountering intriguing and mysterious accounts of the paranormal.

From haunted shipwrecks to the number one most haunted location in the U.S., the eerie nature of these tales sparks wonder about the hidden mysteries in the vast world of the paranormal. Questions arise - could these stories be mere fabrications? Are they signs of mental illness or fear in the person witnessing them? Or is there something else at play?

The enigmatic and chilling nature of these stories leaves us with an insatiable curiosity, prompting contemplation of the unknown and the unexplained, challenging our perception of reality.

As you prepare to close this book, I offer an exciting reminder: Once you step into the world of "Ghost Stories," a captivating journey awaits you, with no turning back. Embrace the thrill of exploration and immerse yourself in the enchanting realm of the supernatural. The mysteries of haunted locations and paranormal encounters will linger in your thoughts, and the shadowy essence surrounding these tales will accompany you into your dreams. I commend your courage in delving into the unknown and unlocking the secrets concealed within these pages.

What makes paranormal stories captivating is that they leave us with more questions, perpetually seeking further discoveries. Embrace your curiosity, and until our next encounter, this is H.J. Tidy, wishing you happy ghost hunting!

ABOUT THE AUTHOR

Meet H.J. Tidy, an exceptional American author renowned for weaving tales of horror, mystery, suspense, and true crime. From a tender age, the enigmatic world of oddities and unsolved mysteries captured his imagination, inspiring a lifelong passion for storytelling.

With an impressive repertoire, H.J. Tidy presents bestselling works that include "Ghost Stories," "True Crime Stories," and "My Creepy Paranormal Stories," all which transport readers on thrilling journeys through the chilling and unknown realms. With a unique ability to enthrall and engage audiences, H.J. Tidy's narratives explore the human psyche's darkest corners, drawing readers into worlds they never knew existed. Embark on an unforgettable literary adventure with this masterful author, where every page turns like a heartbeat at night.

REFERENCES

Dalrymple, L. (2013 October 24). Is Eastern State Penitentiary Really Haunted? NPR.

https://www.npr.org/2013/10/24/232234570/is-eastern-state-penitentiary-really-haunted

Ellis, P. (2020 May 14). The True Story of Al Capone's Later Life, Including How He Died. Men's

Health. https://www.menshealth.com/entertainment/a32461994/al-capone-death-syphilis/

Haunted Prison - The True Haunting of Eastern State Penitentiary. (n.d.). Haunted Places To Go.

https://www.haunted-places-to-go.com/haunted-prison.html

History of Eastern State. (n.d.). Eastern State Penitentiary Historic Site.

https://www.easternstate.org/research/history-eastern-state

Logue, J. (2017 October 25). Is Eastern State Penitentiary really haunted? Metro Philadelphia.

https://metrophiladelphia.com/is-eastern-state-penitentiary-really-haunted/

Nealon, T. (2020 May 19). The Haunted Eastern State Penitentiary. Ghost City Tours.

https://ghostcitytours.com/philadelphia/haunted-philadelphia/eastern-state-penitentiary/

The Prisoners Haunting Eastern State Penitentiary. (2019 June 30). Mysterious Facts.

https://mysteriousfacts.com/prisoners-haunting-eastern-state-penitentiary/

Anas, B. (2020 April 4). Would you spend a night in The Stanley's most haunted rooms? TripSavvy. https://www.tripsavvy. com/the-haunted-stanley-hotel-4108817

Arnett, A. (2018 January 26). Ghosts, doubles and vortices: Revisiting the Stanley Hotel. Brooklyn Paranormal Society. https:// bkps.co/2018/ghosts-doubles-vortices-revisiting-stanley-hotel/

Barber, M. (2014 October 7). Roadtrip to Aspen: Mapping the iconic spots of dumb & dumber. Curbed. https://archive.curbed. com/maps/the-road-to-aspen-mapping-the-iconic-spots-of-dumb-dumber

Beahm, G. W. (1995). Stephen King companion. Andrews and McMeel.

Earls, S. (2019 October 29). Colorado's Stanley Hotel offers plenty of haunted tales. Colorado Springs Gazette. https://gazette. com/life/colorados-stanley-hotel-offers-plenty-of-haunted-tales/article_608df8f4-5c12-57c0-a362-e3dc70103bfa.html

Hicks, K. (2019 October 29). The Stanley Hotel's haunted reputation and how it inspired "The Shining." ABC Action News. https://www.abcactionnews.com/news/national/the-stanley-hotels-haunted-reputation-and-how-it-inspired-the-shining

Karr, M. (2019 May 4). The Stanley Hotel (ghost stories). The Haunted: Debunked. https://thehaunteddebunked.home. blog/2019/05/04/the-stanley-hotel-ghost-stories/

Keith, T. (2021 June 2). You decide: Ghost or curtains? Photo snapped at the Stanley Hotel in Colorado recently. kktv.com. https://www.kktv.com/2021/06/02/you-decide-ghost-or-curtains-photo-snapped-at-the-stanley-hotel-in-colorado-recently/

Nordine, M. (2019 October 23). Is The Stanley Hotel haunted enough to scare a ghost skeptic into believing? The Discoverer. https://www.thediscoverer.com/blog/a-night-at-the-stanley-hotel/XvHyVpKgiwAG5awz

O'Neill, R. (2019 October 28). 10 creepy things you didn't know about the Stanley Hotel. TheTravel. https://www.thetravel.com/stanley-hotel-facts-ghost-creepy/

Weiser, K. (2019). The haunted Stanley Hotel in Estes Park, Colorado. Legendsofamerica.com. https://www.legendsofamerica.com/stanley-hotel-colorado/

Belanger, J. (2014, February 22). The Myrtles Plantation. My Entertainment Holdings.

Carter, M. (2017, October 11). A look inside the most haunted house in America. Country Living. https://www.countryliving.com/life/a45181/myrtles-plantation-louisiana-haunted/

Cellania, M. (2009, October 20). The haunted plantation. Www.mentalfloss.com. https://www.mentalfloss.com/article/23051/haunted-plantation

Fitzhugh, P. (2013). The legend of the Bell Witch of Tennessee. Bellwitch.org. http://www.bellwitch.org/story.htm

Fitzhugh, P. (2020, December 13). A new development in the Bell
　　Witch case. Pat Fitzhugh. https://patfitzhugh.wordpress.
　　com/2020/12/13/a-new-development-in-the-bell-witch-case/

Harrington, R. K. (2020, October 24). The history and the haunting of
　　the Myrtles Plantation. Medium. https://medium.com/
　　exploring-history/the-history-and-the-haunting-of-the-
　　myrtles-plantation-6c1190615f

Haunted Houses. (2006, August 19). Myrtles Plantation bed and
　　breakfast haunted house. Web.archive.org. https://web.
　　archive.org/web/20060819122837/http://www.
　　hauntedhouses.com/states/la/house.htm

Haunted Rooms. (2018). The Myrtles Plantation, St. Francisville,
　　Louisiana. Www.hauntedrooms.com. https://www.
　　hauntedrooms.com/louisiana/haunted-places/haunted-
　　hotels/the-myrtles-plantation

Kermeen, F. (2005). The Myrtles Plantation : the true story of
　　America's most haunted house. Warner Books.

Kreidler, M. (2014, January 1). The "Bell Witch" poltergeist. Skeptical
　　Inquirer. https://skepticalinquirer.org/2014/01/the-bell-
　　witch-poltergeist/

Myrtles Plantation. (2022). Legend of Chloe and ghosts. Www.
　　myrtlesplantation.com. https://www.myrtlesplantation.
　　com/history-and-hauntings/the-legend-of-chloe

Nixon, K. (2017, October 30). Bell Witch lore spins dark tale, but
　　could science explain it all? The Tennessean. https://www.
　　tennessean.com/story/news/local/robertson/2021/10/28/

history-tennessee-bell-witch-could-science-explain-paranormal/8568160002/

Nola Ghosts. (2021, July 31). The haunted Myrtle Plantation. Nolaghosts.com. https://nolaghosts.com/the-haunted-myrtle-plantation/

Solomon, C. (Director). (2005). An american haunting. After Dark Films.

Taylor, T. (2017). Myrtle Plantation legends, lore and lies. American Hauntings. https://www.americanhauntingsink.com/myrtles

Taylor, T., & Wiseheart, D. (2013, October 29). America's most haunted: Myrtles Plantation. Web.archive.org. https://web.archive.org/web/20131029235907/http://www.prairieghosts.com/myrtles.html

Tennessee State Library and Archives. (n.d.). Tennessee myths and legends. Sharetngov.tnsosfiles.com. https://sharetngov.tnsosfiles.com/tsla/exhibits/myth/bellwitch.htm

The Myrtles Plantation. (2022). Take a tour. Www.myrtlesplantation.com. https://www.myrtlesplantation.com/tour

The Shakers. (1988). Living in the shadow of a spirit. Carlyle Records.

Wagner, S. (2017, August 19). The Bell Witch: The real story behind America's best-known poltergeist case. LiveAbout. https://www.liveabout.com/the-bell-witch-2596741

White, R. (Director). (2004). Bell Witch haunting. Willing Hearts Prod.

Wick, D. (1987). The strange true story of the Bell Witch of Tennessee, part 4 of 5. The Mountain Laurel. http://www.mtnlaurel.com/ghost-stories/1233-the-strange-true-story-of-the-bell-witch-of-tennessee-part-4-of-5.html

Wood, S. K. (2018, November 4). Woman shares ghost stories from her "haunted" plantation. AP NEWS. https://apnews.com/article/6f2498d9f64043ffb8e05487f62fa376

Young, N. (2015, October 27). Psychic: I know the real Bell Witch story. USA TODAY. https://www.usatoday.com/story/life/nation-now/2015/10/27/psychic-bell-witch-story/74713998/

(2019 September 22). The Incarcerated Ghosts of Eastern State Penitentiary. Amy's Crypt. https://amyscrypt.com/eastern-state-penitentiary/

Dalrymple, L. (2013 October 24). Is Eastern State Penitentiary Really
    Haunted? NPR.

https://www.npr.org/2013/10/24/232234570/is-eastern-state-
    penitentiary-really-haunted

Darcy, D. (2021 June 6). Wandering The Eerie Eastern State
    Penitentiary. World Adventurists.

https://worldadventurists.com/eastern-state-penitentiary-philadelphia/

Ellis, P. (2020 May 14). The True Story of Al Capone's Later Life,
    Including How He Died. Men's

Health. https://www.menshealth.com/entertainment/a32461994/
    al-capone-death-syphilis/

Haunted Prison - The True Haunting of Eastern State Penitentiary.
    (n.d.). Haunted Places To Go.

https://www.haunted-places-to-go.com/haunted-prison.html

History of Eastern State. (n.d.). Eastern State Penitentiary Historic Site.

https://www.easternstate.org/research/history-eastern-state

J. (2021 February 4). Eastern State Penitentiary: 30 Facts About
    Philadelphia's Haunted Prison.

Thought Catalog. https://thoughtcatalog.com/jeremy-london/
    2018/09/eastern-state-penitentiary/

Logue, J. (2017 October 25). Is Eastern State Penitentiary really
    haunted? Metro Philadelphia.

https://metrophiladelphia.com/is-eastern-state-penitentiary-really-haunted/

Nealon, T. (2020 May 19). The Haunted Eastern State Penitentiary. Ghost City Tours.

https://ghostcitytours.com/philadelphia/haunted-philadelphia/eastern-state-penitentiary/

Punishments, 1780–1925 (n.d.). The Digital Panopticon.

https://www.digitalpanopticon.org/Punishments,_1780-1925

The Prisoners Haunting Eastern State Penitentiary. (2019 June 30). Mysterious Facts.

https://mysteriousfacts.com/prisoners-haunting-eastern-state-penitentiary/

Woodham, C. (2008 October 1). Eastern State Penitentiary: A Prison With a Past. Smithsonian Magazine.

https://www.smithsonianmag.com/history/eastern-state-penitentiary-a-prison-with-a-past-14274660/

Clune, B. (2017). Hollywood Obscura : death, murder, and the paranormal aftermath. Schiffer Publishing Ltd.

Dobson, J. (2018, April 14). The Queen Mary Opens Up Its Haunted Hotel Suite For An Overnight Ghostly Experience. Forbes.

https://www.forbes.com/sites/jimdobson/
2018/04/14/the-queen-mary-opens-up-its-
haunted-hotel-suite-for-an-overnight-ghostly-
experience/?sh=21d9f942575b

Fahrlander, C., & Vickers, N. (2020, October 30).
Haunted Heartland: The Sallie House in
Atchison, KS. KCTV Kansas City. https://
www.kctv5.com/news/local_news/haunted-
heartland-the-sallie-house-in-atchison-ks/
article_f0ad791a-1a26-11eb-bff6-4382ee261acb.html

Fyfe, D. (2014). Overland Limited. The Campo
Santo Quarterly Review, 1(4). The Campo
Santo. https://www.camposanto.com/
quarterlyreview/volume-1/issue-4/overland-limited/

Jones, J. (2011, October 30). San Diego landmark is
ghost hunters' old haunt; Whaley House, an
1850s residence rich in history, is known for
its alleged spectral encounters, which tend to
increase in late October. The Los Angeles Times.

Kroonenberg, S. (2013). Why Hell Stinks of Sulfur :
Mythology and Geology of the Underworld
(A. Brown, Trans.). Reaktion Books.

Lawrence, A. (2017). Paranormal survivors: Validating the struggling middle class. Journal of Popular Film and Television, 45(4), 219–230. https://doi.org/10.1080/01956051.2017.1302922

Maysh, J. (2019, November 16). The Murder House. Medium. https://medium.com/s/story/the-murder-house-8bea26f11e5b

Miller, V. (1873, October 7). Hanging Yankee Jim. Los Angeles Herald. Hanging Yankee Jim

Monif, M. (2020, October 20). A disease often misdiagnosed as madness. Monash Lens. https://lens.monash.edu/@medicine-health/2020/10/20/1381554/autoimmune-encephalitis-when-your-body-attacks-your-brain-and-people-think-youre-going-mad

Naval Historical Society of Australia. (1998, September 18). SS Queen Mary & the loss of HMS Curacoa 1942. Naval Historical Society

7da17414-6d61-4a26-b773-18b9d9c0fac9R01